The Box Car Killer

Barbara Holton

Published by Trellis Publishing, 2021.

THE BOX CAR KILLER

First edition. July 13, 2021.

Copyright © 2021 Barbara Holton.

ISBN: 979-8224737512

Written by Barbara Holton.

THE BOX CAR KILLER

BARBARA HOLTON

Robert Joseph Silveria Junior – The Boxcar Killer

As Bobby lifted his 'gooney stick' axe handle above his head and swung it down with brute force for the third time, he licked his lips as the weapon smashed again into the limp head of his train boxcar companion.

He savoured the moment as he watched the frantic eyes of his victim stammer to a halt and slowly drain of life.

Bobby had become exceptionally good at taking lives – the lives of those who would not be missed.

This is the true story of an extremely brutal and extraordinary serial killer who plagued the United States' busy freight train tracks for some fifteen years. Over the decade and a half between 1981 and 1996, Robert Joseph Silveria Junior's horrific and truly terrifying killing spree led him to ultimately take the lives of some 28 fellow travellers until being finally apprehended.

Robert Silveria Junior is unique in many ways.

His uncontrollable temper and lust for killing was indeed insatiable and unquenchable and, one could argue the tell-tale signs of his growing obsession with death, had been evident early on in his life. But what made Robert stand out just that little bit more, was his charm and wit. He thrived on relationships and came across as the friend or boyfriend you wouldn't hesitate to take home to meet your parents.

Robert Joseph Silveria Junior was born on the 3rd of March, 1959. He was to be the second child of four, with one sister and two brothers. In later life, Robert would also gain a half-brother due to his parent's eventual divorce.

Robert grew up in Redwood City, California which bustled with business given its port location in the San Francisco Bay Area. Redwood City would also become a thriving part of the Silicon Valley boom in later years where opportunities quadrupled and people learnt to live the high life. But for Robert, he and his family would not be privy to such enjoyments – a reasonable middle-class lifestyle yes; but not an enjoyable one by any account.

Both of Robert's parents were hard working, with his father, Robert Senior, working as a Supervisor at the local airport and his mother, taking on a job in an airline catering business.

By all accounts, the Silveria's were a typical American suburban family but, as Robert Junior grew older, his behavior and attitude to life took a dark turn.

At the age of just 11 years old, Robert had begun to continuously skip school and was even caught experimenting with drugs. But little did anyone realize that this handsome child, with his slightly curled light brown hair and piercing blue eyes, would become more than just a young teenage menace.

Robert was tall for his age - which possibly gave him the confidence to hang around with other like-minded, yet older, local bikers. Despite being well-liked and a known troublemaker, Robert enjoyed his freedom as a rogueing nomad.

By the tender age of 12, he had been caught robbing his neighbours' home. But, instead of feeling an inkling of remorse following the rather harsh words and punishment handed down by his father, Robert instead, took his revenge on the family next door. Seeking swift retribution for his received penance, Robert bludgeoned the family's much-loved pet to death as a form of retribution.

Robert would later retell of the brutal and physical abuse he had often received from his father as being the trigger point to his life of crime.

With wildness in his heart and a stubborn attitude toward conformity, it was not long before Robert Silveria Junior was eventually expelled from school; but not before at least receiving his High School Diploma.

Exasperated with his continued aggression and his now unfailing habitual thirst for drugs, it was becoming very apparent that Robert - Bobby to his friends – had absolutely no intention of following any rules to life. Robert wanted desperately to do his own thing and, with his ever-uncontrollable temper and rage taking its toll on the family, it is somewhat understandable that Robert's parents began to slowly distance themselves from him.

Yet despite the continued verbal abuse and physical hostility they received from their son, Robert Senior still attempted one last time to steer his son in the right direction. Calling in a favour, Robert Sr managed to secure a job for his troubled son as a baggage handler at the airport he worked for as a Supervisor.

But just as he feared, it was not long before Robert Jr. had been caught stealing and fired from his job. Bobby's insatiable drug and alcohol habit had taken its full grip on the young man who now sought any way to come up with the money to keep his habit going.

Stealing became the norm for Bobby. It would not be long before stealing would metamorphosize into murder.

By taking on some odd jobs and helping out at a nearby tattoo parlour in San Jose and, linked to the motorbiking community, Robert Jr. initially managed to finance his drug use. But as his habit became more uncontrollable, Robert again resorted to burglary and theft, shocking his family by stealing his own father's truck and eventually serving almost a year in prison for his crime.

Robert Jr was paroled in 1980 at the age of 21.

But now, with his parents no longer welcoming him to the new home they had moved into with Robert Jr's siblings, Bobby sought refuge and a roof over his head by his uncle in Quincy Plumas County. His uncle remains the only member of Robert Jr's family who has stood by him, even giving us some insight into how Bobby had behaved during his stay with him.

Robert's uncle, Lloyd Chapin, a biker himself, lived above the auto parts store he both owned and worked at. Whilst staying with his uncle, Bobby earned money by working at the outlet thrift store for the poor, often going house to house to seek donations from unsuspecting locals.

Bobby also continued with his real passion in life, his tattooing, which he offered to local biker gangs he had befriended. His associates recall that Bobby was not only a soft-spoken guy with rugged appeal, but was also quite a hard-working young man.

Chapin recalls, "He was quiet and well-mannered," but, "he also shot heroin". And as his uncle would further explain, Bobby was like an innocent boy scout to him and someone who could never be responsible for all the murders that took place, "He would be the last person in the world you would think who would be doing what he did".

During his time with his uncle, Robert met and married his first wife at the age of 25 on the 19th of May 1984. But just as so many of his failed relationships and inability to socially connect, the wedded bliss didn't last long for the couple, with the new bride leaving him a year later in November 1985.

Interestingly, this was also around the same time that a local race car driver was found dead. Police had initially chalked up the death to suicide, but with three further people found murdered in the area and, the local airport where Bobby had briefly worked as a caretaker recently burgled, detectives began to take more notice of this distinct escalation of crime in the county.

In 1986, and now aged 27, Bobby briefly reunited with his estranged wife and the couple brought a beautiful daughter into the world - a new start for them all as a family.

But like so many things in Bobby's life, this postcard happiness was to be short lived. Not only did he have a crumbling relationship on his hands, but Bobby also argued and fell out with his uncle in spectacular style.

Leaving his shackles of normal life behind him, Bobby took his leave of everyone and the town of Stockton in 1986.

He was free to do whatever he wanted to do.

He was free from the controls and constraints of a typical normal life.

He could finally breathe.

What his uncle and wife did not know, was that Bobby had already killed a man when he was just aged 22 and had got away with it.

Throughout his youth, Bobby had enjoyed talking to people that led a truly nomadic existence - whether self-inflicted or just by choice.

Homeless people - men who themselves, had been let down by the system in some fashion; suffering with mental health problems; unable to function in the normal world. These were the men that inspired Robert.

He was just like them. He himself, was unable to live a normal existence.

The men who interested Bobby the most were ex-Vietnam veterans and he had an unhealthy fascination with them.

Robert Jr. would love nothing more than to hear all about their broken lives.

the Veterans would tell their tragic tales of how, as just young men themselves, they were called upon by the US government to participate in a war that they knew could never be won. They would talk of how proud they had felt to serve their county and be a part of something they believed was for the greater good. They would discuss the trauma they endured; surrounded by the never-ending violence; the killings that they themselves, had to carry out on nameless faces.

It was life or fight or be killed. And many were taken in the horrific bloodshed that lay under the banner of righteous war.

For the veterans, the hell they endured was the scariest environment ever imaginable. Even though many survived without physical injury, the torment of their actions would never leave them.

As Bobby savoured every morsel of their appalling stories, the veterans would tell of how they had thought they would return to a hero's welcome, but now they were mere begging nuisance on the street; the conveniently forgotten few; the troublemakers.

Robert was home. He was the nuisance; the forgotten; the troublemaker.

Robert began a new chapter in his life; a free spirit with no one to answer to but himself. He started living in camps, or jungles located along the extensive American freight train tracks. He was a hobo who jumped on and off the bulky slow-moving trains at no expense. He travelled up and down America, staying in the boxcars as he pleased.

His only problem – money.

When welfare cheques and food stamps weren't enough to trade with fellow rail riders to support his drug addiction, Bobby started to steal from fellow passengers who were sleeping or had passed out from overdoses of alcohol or drugs. He would happily steal anything of worth; anything to trade and anything he wanted to wear. Backpackers were also using the freight trains as a means of free travel, making them easy pickings for Bobby – who now carried the renowned name of "Side-track Bob".

At aged 30, Bobby was to kill again.

In 1989 he murdered Anthony Garcia in West Sacramento California, using his signature weapon, a "gooney stick", which was a self-fashioned axe handle he used to quickly stun and paralyze his victims.

Bobby enjoyed kicking his victims faces with his own heavy boots, stamping on their heads. He would then viciously take to pummelling their faces with his three-foot axe handle, often stabbing at them too. He seemed to take pleasure in his kills and took his time until the victims succumbed to their frenzied attackers' brutality.

Bobby was brash to say the least, leaving the bloody corpses on the trains until they were eventually found. It became all to easy for him to evade capture because he could quickly distance himself from his victims, travelling hundreds of miles away from every crime scene.

In November 1990 and now thirty-one years old, Robert Jr married his second wife and joined the organised and highly dangerous criminal gang, the FTRA (Freight Train Raiders of America). Known for their distribution of narcotics through using the ease and speed of the railroad networks, the FTRA also had a strict code that had to be obeyed - something Robert wasn't used to.

The notorious gang members consisted of far-right-wing and white men who had deep convictions and strong beliefs in the return of an Arian Race regime. This group believed themselves to be of a superior race, similar to the sadistic concepts borne out of Nazi Germany. The FTRA organisation originated within the biking community and disgruntled Vietnam vets, who had become disillusioned by what they saw as their country's lack lustre laws. So, they made their own.

Robert instantly took to their philosophies and criminal activity, stealing mainly from those high up on the vulnerable chain. Despite some Railroad officials claiming that the FTRA just doesn't exist, law enforcement has tried to investigate them over the past decade with little to no success. They have often been referred to as 'bikers without bikes' and 'outlaws of the tracks.'

A retired Police Officer, Bob Grandinetti began his investigation into the warped organization as early as the 1980s as a result of a number of unexplained deaths and bodies that had been found in and around the railway tracks. For the inspector, this sudden surge, could not be put down to suicide alone. More sinisterly, he discovered extensive similarities to the inflicted wounds and means of death on many of the victims found along the railway tracks between Spokane and Sandpoint, Idaho. Often victims had been robbed leaving no identification and with their jackets pulled over their faces to disguise the brutal wounds and gruesome facial and cranial injuries. Sometimes their trousers had been pulled down to their ankles, almost to shame them in death although there were no signs of sexual abuse on any of the victims.

Roberts Silveria Junior was totally out of control by now. With his extremely short fuse and desire for blood now being his only driving force, he simply could not get enough.

The murders would start in 1981 and finish some fifteen years later, as he worked his way through the States of California, Oregon, Utah, Arizona, Kansas, Washington and Florida. This maniac had turned into a one-man plague.

His method was an easy one: he would befriend vulnerable men of any age with his friendly experienced approach; offering to share cigarettes and booze with them; advice was given freely, and reassurance given until his chosen victim became all too comfortable with him. In his own subtle way, Robert Jr was also able to find out where his intended victim was heading and what they were carrying in their back packs.

At this point, Robert Jr would later admit to flying into an uncontrollable rage which could only be quenched, in his mind, when he had finally bludgeoned the victims to death. This was when he would feel some relief.

Then, rummaging through their pitiful belongs, he would steal anything of value, even a new pair of boots that one of his victims wore. New coats; cash; it was all his for the taking.

In March 1996 a railroad officer in Roseville, Placer County made the most gruesome of discoveries. Finding two dead bodies in a boxcar whilst going about his daily duties, the railroad officer was left tormented by the hideous scene. Both corpses had been placed face down and their heads covered with their jackets. The scene was a total blood bath with the victims having been attacked so violently in the face and head that they were barely recognizable as human beings.

The railroad officer immediately called the local police station in Oregon State where Detective Michael Quakenbush was stationed.

Taking the call, Detective Quakenbush immediately sped to the crime scene where he found the brutally mutilated bodies of William Avis Petit, a 39-year-old known hobo, as well as the 24-year-old Michael Andrew Clites, a drifter from Portland.

The Detective immediately knew this was the work of one sadistic slayer. Trawling through CCTV footage from the area and on the cameras overlooking the tracks at the station, Detective Quakenbush spotted Robert Silveria Jr leaving the boxcar and scene of the crime just moments after the horrific deaths.

Immediately sending out an emergency police bulletin as well as presenting Robert Silveria Jr's picture on television, police made an urgent appeal to the public for their help in the apprehension of this dangerous man.

A local bar attender called the police, explaining that she had seen both Robert and the victim Michael, drinking alcohol together only a few days earlier and explained how the pair had seemed very friendly with each other and well acquainted.

It was not long before Robert Joseph Silveria Jr. was spotted walking along the tracks near the makeshift FTRA camp and swiftly apprehended by Police. He was taken immediately to Placer County Jail where he was put into an isolation cell.

During their search of his clothing and the possessions Robert Jr had on him at the time of his arrest, police discovered William Avis Petit's Social Security Card, prompting Detective Quakenbush to begin his formal interview with the suspect.

Detective Quakenbush found Robert Jr to be both calm and well spoken - even softly spoken for a man of his size and reputation. He was indeed eager to tell the detective all about his life of brutal crimes - almost with too much enthusiasm. The detective at one point in the interview asked Robert what name he went by on the tracks, he replied, *"Sidecar Bob of course!"* He told the Detective how Michael had made him angry on that fateful night and how he had shouted to Michael that he was never getting out of that Boxcar alive. Without so much as a slight hesitancy, Robert Silveria Jr then began to describe Michael's brutal death at his hands in terrifying detail. Robert explained how he had proceeded to kick Michael in the face before unleashing his full force on the trembling man. Coldly, Robert Jr had turned his attention to the unfortunate drifter who had been cowering in the same boxcar as them. He enjoyed taking two lives that day – and doing so with so much force and violence.

During his interview with the detective, Robert eventually confessed to killing around 28 men at least he had thought. He also disclosed one location of interest, Albany.

After interviewing Robert, Detective Quakenbush made an urgent call to his colleague In the Albany Police Department, a Detective Bill Palmini. It was not long before Detective Palmini sat in front of the cold and calculating Robert Joseph Silveria Jr.

Bill Palmini, who retired from the force in 2003 recalls his time spent interviewing Robert Silveria. Bill had been completely dumbfounded at how Robert had come across in his interview with him saying, *"I was amazed when I met him, he was looking at me, smiling... but beneath the veneer of charm there was a seething rage."* The detective recalled how specific and detailed Robert's testimony and account of certain murders had been, even revealing details that had never been released to the public.

Robert Jr spoke of how he had killed one of his victim's dog, as it was drawing to much attention with its barking and howling. Another confession revealed a different victim had new boots on, so he had stolen them but revealed that one of the boots had a double heel. His recollection of his victims and accounts of their deaths were truly astonishing.

Robert would also confess to the murder of James "JC" Mclean, another homeless man aged 50 years old, who was found near Albany California. Palmini had taken it upon himself to make his life a personal crusade to unmask the operations of the FTRA and its criminal activity on the freight trains of America. He has not only written a book about there exploits, but along with other police officers, public health workers and a works crew, managed to also eventually gain permission to bulldoze the site where Siveria's victim, James Mclean was found. The dark murderous place is no longer a jungle camp for the outlaws of the rails now, but has been turned into a public car parking lot. All signs of this once horrific death scene have now been erased.

In the time he spent with Robert Jr, Palmini probed to better understand what had driven Robert to kill in the way he had. "Take a number", was Bobby's short and sharp reply. Asking him to explain further, Robert told Palmini of a time he recalled when he was a young teenager. He had tried to seek help at a mental Health Facility, the Vancouver Mental Health Agency and explained how he had been trying to overcome his erratic behavior, drug addiction and anger issues. Having eventually plucked up the courage to find the right help he recalled how, whilst explaining this to the receptionist at the hospital front desk, the nurse had coldly replied, *"Take a number and wait your turn, everybody has problems!"*

Robert would never forget this statement and he would never seek help again.

Another Officer who interviewed Robert, was police officer Wade Harper who was attached to the Emeryville Police Department. During their interview together, Harper had asked Robert what his weapon of choice had been. Robert told him that he used an axe handle and then with pen and paper, proceeded to draw it. Robert drew an oval shape to show the axe head and a three-foot pole which he said was made of oak. Robert then signed and dated his artwork and presented it to the horrified officer.

In 1998, two years after his arrest the trial of the serial killer known as Robert Joseph Silveria Junior began in Oregon. Robert Jr would only plead guilty to two murders, but was suspected of killing at least 14 other men at the time. In total, the villainous murderer would later confess to around 28 other murders.

Robert Silveria Jr was given a plea bargain, avoiding the death penalty and thus only being given a double life sentence without opportunity for parole. Quite ironic for a man who killed so many men in such brutal fashion

In Kansas he was convicted of killing Charles Randall Boyd and in Florida, found guilty for the murder of Willie Clark. Robert Silveria Jr is serving a double life sentence for murder in the 1st degree at Wyoming Medium Correctional Institution in Torrington, Wyoming. In prison he works as the head cook and also offers help to fellow prisoners in the inhouse support system. The WMCI correctional facility is an intake centre for men who have not been sentenced to death but have been convicted of serious crimes.

A friend of Silveria Junior, "Guitar Whitey" a fellow hobo, insisted Robert was the kind of guy you would have come to live with you and is adamant that Bobby couldn't be capable of the murders he was accused of. Much like his uncle had believed, Bobby had a charm and calm about him on the surface that was easily mistaken as solid social skills.

Thinking back on the potential opportunities to change the path that Robert Silveria Jr's life had taken, it is difficult to define if sometimes killers are just born that way or indeed, is a construction of learnt childhood behavior and experiences in life. It is unfortunately now all too common for one to blame others for their actions, almost a fashion for a defendant.

For Robert Jr, his upbringing did not seem to have been all that bad. He had grown up in a reasonable middle-class home in a middle-class town. Yes, his father had been tough and probably sometimes physically rough with his young son. But all people who have fallen victim to such treatment behind the closed doors of their family homes, do not become brutal murderers.

Anger is anger if you let it. Murder is murder if you commit it.

THE RED ROCK KILLER

Roger Fain is reaching that age when most Americans are thinking of retirement. He is sixty five in 2019, and should be looking forward to a life of leisurely commitments, perhaps time with the grand kids, or enjoying his interests and hobbies.

But, instead, the future Fain can see consists of four concrete walls, unpleasant smells and the ever present threat of violence. It is very unlikely that he will set foot in the free world again; instead an old age inside the prison system beckons, which will surely hold him until, unmissed and forgotten, he passes on and his place is taken by the next felon in the unending cycle of US crime.

It is hard not to spend time reflecting on how Roger Fain might feel as he approaches this milestone in his life. Does he regret his past misdemeanors, holding some form of guilt for what he has done? According to Dan Anderson, ex husband of one of the woman alleged, but not proven, to have been a victim of Fain's crimes, he does not.

'There's no emotion, no motive. Those are the scary ones,' said Anderson after Fain's second conviction for murder. Even his attorney, the court appointed Mike Davis, finds it hard to offer up much in the way of defense.

'It does not sadden me to see this.' Davis said of his client's conviction. 'I certainly have no obligation to him anymore.' The then District Attorney of Williamson County John Bradley expressed not the slightest regret about the fact that Fain will die in prison for his crimes.

'That really puts the nail in the coffin,' he said.

Maybe Fain continues to see himself as a victim of a mis-carriage of justice. He has staunchly maintained his innocence of involvement in the deaths of three women, including Darlene Anderson. Twice, he has taken his case to the court of appeal, unsuccessful at even gaining a review of his convictions on both occasions.

But, when that evidence is weighed up, it is hard to make a case for his defense.

Roger Eugene Fain was born in 1954 in Florida. The Sunshine State seemed to glow elsewhere to young Fain, and following a difficult upbringing, his first serious brush with the law occurred when he was just 16. 1970 was a difficult time to be young in America. The rock and roll revolution, led by Elvis Presley, had changed perceptions of and about teenagers forever and the hippy culture helped to cause confusion in growing minds.

The threat of Vietnam hung over young men like an avenging angel – but for all that, this was the baby boomer generation and in many ways Americans had never had it so good. Such bounties, though, passed the young Roger Fain by and he was accused of raping a 33 year old woman while still, technically, a boy. On that occasion, the courts were lenient, but over the next two decades Fain became of regular interest to law enforcers.

Conviction after conviction followed in these years; burglary and robbery were his most frequent offenses, but charges of kidnapping also occurred.

In 1990 he decided to leave Florida, seeking a new start in Texas. It didn't last long. In the Spring of 1991 Fain was arrested in Cameron County, on the southernmost tip of the state. The charges laid against him were among the most serious he had faced to date. Kidnapping and aggravated assault. However, when it came to court, it was the lesser charge of false imprisonment which saw him convicted.

But luck, for once, shone on Fain. He was sent to prison in Texas in 1991, but was paroled much earlier than he might have expected, and found himself free in 1992. Chris Mealy, a member of the Texas Board of Pardons and Paroles from 1987 to 1990 was clear that Fain was fortunate to be released.

'Fain was a direct result of there not being enough space to keep him long enough,' he said. But while the consequences of overcrowded prisons might have been beneficial to Roger Fain, for two, maybe three, young women and their families they would lead to devastating consequences.

It is easy to picture Fain as a kind of down at heel, fringes of society type semi vagabond. Nothing could be further than the truth. More, he adopted the looks of a 70s film star, albeit one slightly gone to seed. His long, flowing dark brown locks, tanned body and defined chest gave way to the beginnings of a pot belly, but for all this he seemed to exert a kind of fascination for women. Later, when on trial for the worst crimes imaginable that could be conducted against a female – rape and murder – women flocked to support him in court.

To John Bradley, however, the attraction was hard to understand. 'There was something charismatic about him, to some women at least,' he said. Fain also had a reputation as a ladies' man, a smooth talking Lothario who saw women melt in his company. Mick Davis is also bemused by his attraction for the opposite sex.

'He had this entourage of women who followed him all the way,' he said.

The picture that emerges of the Roger Fain of the mid to late 1980s is of a man with a magnetic appeal to certain women. One who happily engages in multiple concurrent relationships. A petty criminal who, at times, strays into far more serious and violent offenses against the opposite sex.

Then, on June 1st 1987 a woman's body was discovered at her home in Arlington, Texas. Linda Sue Donahew was 41; she had been strangled and stabbed to death in her own house. Sexual assault had also taken place.

Hair found in Linda's hands suggested that she had put up a fight, but the nature of her death was strange and perverted. She was found completely nude, and it appeared as though whoever had killed her had cut, rather than torn, off her clothes; an act that suggests cold calculation rather than any momentary loss of control.

The murder turned even more bizarre when it became apparent that Linda had paintings on her body; they had been drawn using her own blood. Although, along with the hair found grasped in the victim's hand, semen was found on her body, back then in the late 1980s forensic science was in its infancy, and there was no way of testing likely culprits to identify the killer.

Police took whatever information they could. They knew that the 41 year old had, at one stage, had a brief fling with a younger man, who they identified as Roger Fain. Witnesses reported that they had seen an old white pick up truck parked near to Linda's home. Police knew that Roger Fain owned a 1976 pick up truck. It happened to be white.

Other witnesses described potential attackers – men who had been seen around the area in the hours leading up to Linda's death. Artists' impressions were produced, and anybody looking closely would have noticed a similarity between a drawing of a tallish, thick set man with long wavy hair – a bit of a 1970s throwback in many ways. A drawing of a man with similar features to that one time, brief, boyfriend of the victim. Roger Fain.

In the cold, dispassionate light of many years after the crime, such evidence seems hard to ignore. It appears almost negligent that police failed to identify Fain as a suspect. A quick check on his history would have revealed a man who served time for the false imprisonment of women, who had moved up from Florida where he left behind a record of criminal activity, including some sexual attacks.

But we are talking about the late 1980s. The police worked differently. Communication between different forces was less good. However it occurred, Roger Fain slipped through the net. He was not even listed as a suspect.

Time passed and Linda Donahew's murder moved from big news, through just becoming one of many priorities, to an investigation that was going nowhere to, eventually, storage in the cold case cellars of the Arlington Police department.

Life moved on. Roger Fain continued to attract women, he continued to sport his long wavy hair, his open shirts, a look that went out of date many years before. It didn't seem to matter. Girlfriend followed girlfriend, acquaintance succeeded acquaintance.

Until, that is, 1994, when tragedy struck once more. This time, a double tragedy. In the space of just a month two women went missing. The locations this time were two cities close together. Round Rock, at the time a small town with a population of around 30000 inhabitants, and the State capital of Austin.

Round Rock was to undergo a massive growth following the opening of the giant Dell headquarters later in the year. But during the summer in question, Williamson County saw other matters occupying people's thoughts. OJ Simpson's arrest was captivating the entire nation. Of course, failed forensic processes would play a significant part in the athlete's acquittal for double homicide. That was seven years after the Donahew murder, but gave credence to the police's view that, back then, the collection, analysis and storage of forensic evidence was just not advanced enough to secure convictions.

Locally in Williamson County choices for school text books were causing widespread anguish between those with a more fundamentalist view of life, and those who saw things differently. Yet when it occurred, the death of two women was enough to push OJ Simpson and school board book choices to the back of people's attention.

The two women in question were Sandra Dumont, a 39 year old from Austin who worked as a card dealer at a local nightclub, and, a month before her, Darlene Anderson, the mother of a twelve year old daughter, who worked at Austin Semiconductor had also gone missing. Her record there was exemplary, and when she failed to turn up for her shift, colleagues were immediately concerned.

Other than living under twenty miles apart, there was little to connect the two disappearances at the outset. Although, they did share something in common. Something unconnected at first, but later of great significance. Both victims had held relationships with a certain Roger Eugene Fain. John Bradley later put the fact into context.

'Both of the women,' he explained, commenting on how the crimes were connected 'they did have relationships with him.'

Darlene Anderson went missing on June 27th 1994. By July 4th the local newspaper was reporting her disappearance, not least because it was so out of character.

'This is just too damned weird,' said her ex-husband at the time, who lived in Midland, a town on the other side of the State. Then, when by the middle of the month no progress had been made into solving her disappearance, hundreds of local people – and some from farther afield - set out to help. A two day search, with some helpers on horseback, ensued. Among the good citizens taking part was one man with something to hide – Roger Fain was there, searching for the woman many believe he raped and killed.

That assistance, or whatever we might call it, would in the end play a significant role in the murderer's downfall. Police are aware that killers often like to return to the scene of their crime, and to be involved in the investigations into it. This can be for many reasons: a sense of pride for the fuss they have caused and the attention which they can claim to have created; a macabre desire to keep the memory of their act as close to the forefront of their minds as possible; a wish to keep a close eye on the investigation, to know how near the crime is to being solved and, in this case, perhaps offer something to put the investigators off the scent.

Fain, forty by now and working as a construction worker, lived in a duplex that was just a half a mile from Anderson's home. We can only speculate as to what motivated him to participate in the search, but in doing so he placed himself in the position of becoming part of a painstaking police investigation into the backgrounds of all those who came to help.

Seven hundred names were taken down, and slowly, methodically, police researched into such criminal history any of those participants might hold. Officers Dan LeMay and Mary Ryle of the Round Rock Police Department were behind that lengthy trawl. Eventually, they reached the name of Roger Fain, and the police officers found a history that prompted further consideration.

Mike Davis recalls the incident:

'Everybody that participated in the search,' he said, 'they took their name and did a search of their criminal history.'

Meanwhile, on July 25th, Dumont too went missing. The link between the two victims was not immediately apparent, but that changed in early August. An Austin Police Sergeant, Michael Phillips, discovered the remains of two bodies. Dental records identified the women as Darlene Anderson and Sandra Dumont. The two were discovered just a couple of hundred feet apart, on private property - a cow pasture – close to Louis Henna Boulevard. The discovery site was later earmarked for housing development.

Phillips also discovered that Sandra's car, a grey 1980 Toyota Corolla, had been found nearby. The chances of two women going missing, then being discovered so close together, being mere coincidence was too hard to swallow. That they shared a boyfriend, and that boyfriend had a long list of criminal convictions was also too strong a clue to ignore.

Now, it was just a case of proving Fain's guilt.

He was arrested in the middle of August – just three weeks after Sandra Dumont had gone missing. From the outset, the prosecutors seemed clear that they had caught their man. Fain's bond was set at a whopping $5million. The Justice of the Peace responsible, Jimmy Bitz, set a record high for Williamson County.

A District Judge who became involved in the case, Ken Anderson, explained the reasoning behind the impossibly large figure.

'The community was justifiably concerned,' he said. 'When you have two women who disappear and get murdered, it is disconcerting.'

One of the strongest pieces of evidence against Fain gave an insight into how at least one of the victims, Sandra Dumont, had suffered. When her body was found, it was discovered that her jaw had been broken. The wound was consistent with having been struck by a rounded object, something like a fist.

Roger Fain had a medical record for the end of July. He had attended Seton Hospital in Austin with an injury. Somehow, he had fractured his hand. Doctor's described that injury as a 'boxer's fracture'. The coincidence between the two events was yet another, as John Bradley might have put it, 'nail in his coffin.' However, it had not been a physical blow to the jaw that had killed the victim, police discovered that she had been shot in the head.

Anderson's death had been caused also by injury to the head, although she had been killed with blows from a blunt instrument.

It seems as though Roger Fain had murdered three women. Who knows, there could be more. At this point, however, he had not been associated with the death of Linda Donahew, and had only been charged with the murder of Sandra Dumont. While police and prosecutors were not looking for anybody else in relation to the death of Darlene Anderson, they had insufficient evidence to charge the Florida born man.

Meanwhile, in Williamson County, the news of the murders were on everybody's lips, In fact Mike Davis recalls that the Judge, John Carter, decided to move the trial to Tyler in East Texas, because of the publicity in the women's home region.

'It's almost like the Henry Lee Lucas level of publicity,' he said. Lucas was once thought to have been America's most prolific serial killer. He had been charged with eleven homicides a decade before, but had confessed (unreliably, in many cases) to around 3000 murders.

At the trial, the jury were out for only twelve hours before returning a verdict of guilty to first degree homicide. As much as a smooth talker as Fain might have been, nothing he said could explain away his injured hand and the broken jaw of his victim.

Later, when he would be charged with the murder of Linda Donahew, the evidence would be stronger. But this was the 1990s, the OJ Simpson era. Times were different, although the number of years that passed between his two convictions were relatively few.

Mike Davis puts the changes in evidence into context.

'From a technical standpoint, it was a very interesting case,' he says of the conviction in Tyler. 'Up in Fort Worth (where the second trial took place) they had DNA evidence. Here, it turned on the broken hand.'

However, despite the finding of guilt, Fain continued to argue that he was responsible for nothing more than being an acquaintance of both Darlene Anderson and Sandra Dumont. He had not, he continued to protest, killed either of them.

He was interviewed by the local newspaper in September 1994 from his cell in Williamson County Jail, saying: 'I'm not crazy or insane. I'm not a psycho killer, or a kidnapping rapist from hell.' Of course, the jury, based on the evidence with which they were presented, thought differently.

Twelve years later, Fain was serving his time, quietly, with any chance of parole still eighteen years away. Then, the past was to catch up with him once again. Fain was resident at the Eastham Prison Unit in Loveday, when 200 miles to the North West, in Fort Worth, breakthroughs were being made in a murder investigation which had lain dormant in the police department's cold case section for approaching two decades.

Twenty years previously, and twenty miles away from the Police Department headquarters where cold case investigators made their break through, Linda Donahew's sister, Bonnie Bishop, had made that gruesome discovery.

It was she who had walked into the home they shared and found the naked body of Linda lying on the floor, stabbed and strangled, murdered and painted with her own blood. It was, however, the semen that had been removed from his victim's vagina that secured Fain's conviction. The cold case investigators responsible had sent the sample away for analysis in the summer of 2015, and a few months later they had received a match. The results had come from a nationwide data base created to record the DNA of known offenders. A warrant was obtained to take a further sample of DNA from Fain, and this confirmed that it was his DNA that had been found on Linda's body.

In that special way police have of speaking when they do not wish to state too much information, but reveal plenty, Arlington Police Sergeant Mark Simpson offered up the following details to the waiting press.

'The suspect is a state inmate serving life in prison for the 1994 shooting death of his ex-girlfriend, Sandra Dumont, Austin. The former Dallas man also has a lengthy history or crimes against women across Florida and Texas, including kidnapping and aggravated sexual assault.'

A short search on the online files would quickly identify Roger Eugene Fain as the man in question.

However, for Bonnie Bishop, the news was strangely comforting. 'I knew deep down in my heart that whoever did this couldn't know my sister well,' she said. 'If you knew her, you couldn't have done that to her. I felt from the very start he was a criminal, a serial killer.'

Once they finally, twenty years after the crime, had found their suspect, police were able to put together the events leading up to Linda's savage murder.

Suddenly, a corpse was able to become a person once more. Rather than just a victim, people read about the true Linda. The real estate agent who had a passion for renovating houses and selling them on. A woman with a love for country and Western music and a deep care for animals, especially her horse, whom she had called 'Hero.' She drove a Corvette and was an independent woman, who enjoyed her freedom.

Linda had a close and loving family, two sisters and two brothers. All, of course, were devastated by both the timing and the manner of her death.

Police pieced together the short lived relationship between killer and victim. They believe that the two had met at a bar in the affluent south west area of Arlington close to where she lived. That initial meeting in John B's bar on Arlington Lane had led to a brief period of dating, but nothing serious had developed.

And now, with the DNA evidence in their possession, police were able to see the significance of the white pick up truck spotted close to Linda's home, they saw the likeness between the artist's impression of the chief suspect and Fain's own appearance.

The cold case officers in charge of the investigation were Jim Ford and John Bell. When they travelled to Fain's prison, he refused to speak to them without an attorney. The officers saw this as further proof of his guilt.

'Once this case started coming together, it was like an avalanche,' Simpson said.

When the case came to trial, in December 2007, prosecutors initially sought the death penalty, but soon dropped this line. It was clear that, should he be found guilty (which seemed inevitable), Fain would be facing an indirect death sentence anyway. Any sentence would be stacked on top of his existing conviction, in other words, he would not begin to serve his time for this crime until he had completed the sentence for the murder of Sandra Dumont. Even though laws in force in 1987 would come into play, meaning that Fain would be eligible for parole after fifteen years, he would already be an old man by the time that sentence began. At least fifteen years after that? Well, it was unlikely he would live that long. There was next to no chance that he would ever be released from prison.

'If he's convicted in this case, there is no way he's ever going to get out,' admitted his attorney, J. Warren St. John.

With the evidence of his white pick up truck, his description, his relationship to the victim and, crucially, the DNA evidence found on Linda's body, the evidence against Fain was overwhelming. The only information that could fall in his favor might be found in the handful of hair Linda had torn from her attacker's head.

As results from the DNA tests on the hair were awaited, St. John clutched at whatever straws were available to him.

'We hope it's beneficial to our client,' he said.

It wasn't; the jury took less than an hour to return a verdict of guilty. After sentencing, John Bradley felt his initial judgements on Roger Fain had been confirmed. 'I would put Fain and Michael Moore together,' he said, linking Fain to the killer of a pregnant woman, and a suspect in the murder of a teenager.

Dan Anderson agreed. 'I think they would probably be in the same category. People who either need to be executed or put in prison for the rest of their life.'

Fain continues to protest his innocence, despite the overwhelming evidence against him. He has twice attempted to have the conviction for the murder of Sandra Donahew overturned, seeking further analysis of the DNA in the samples of hair the victim was found clutching. This has never been identified.

In both cases, appeal court judges refused to even allow his case to be considered. Roger Fain, it seems, will serve his sentence.

Dan Anderson has never known for sure who killed his ex-wife, the mother of his daughter. However certain he is in his head that Roger Fain is her killer, he has not had that confirmed. Closure, such as is ever possible in such tragedy, has come more fully to Bonnie Bishop.

Following Fain's conviction for her sister's murder, she said:

'Hopefully my sister can rest in peace now. I always knew somehow, someday they would find him. It was a hard thing to understand what happened,' she recalled. 'She was so young, and her life was all ahead of her. He took our lives too. Finally, after 18 years, we have some kind of closure.'

But forgiveness, however, remains a distant prospect.

'I want him to pay for what he did to my sister.'

As those walls confront him, day after day after day, never changing, she can be assured that Roger Fain is paying for the crimes he committed.

BIKINI KILLER

DAVID MORRISEY

There are few serial killers quite as successful as Charles Sobhraj. Fluent in several languages, extremely intelligent, and known for his irresistible charms with women, Sobhraj lived a life of nonstop thievery, murder, drugs, and scandal. His unstoppable resourcefulness allowed him to escape authorities half a dozen times through luck, timing, and even what seems to be a strange sense of fate. His favorite means of getting what he wanted involved befriending his victims through faked favors and gifts only to eventually drug and loot, or sometimes murder, them. Known as the "Bikini Killer", a name given to him after he brutally drowned two women and left their bodies dressed in similar bikinis, Charles Sobhraj stretched his crimes across an entire continent and three separate countries. Along the way, he gathered to himself many loyal followers, amassing a sort of cult-like group of acolytes that helped him scam, murder, and steal from nearly everyone he met. Narcissistic and carefree, Sobhraj never took being arrested and convicted of his crimes as a reason to stop. Instead, he routinely bribed guards and fellow inmates so that he could live his days in prison in the lap of luxury. He cheerfully recounts his actions to any news reporter or author that will give him the time of day, although he is careful never to say in so many words that he committed any murders. In addition to his more famous nickname, Sobhraj has also been dubbed "the Serpent". As of today, he has been convicted for only one of his believed 12-24 murders, and he is awaiting charges for a second.

This is the biography of serial killer and con artist Charles Sobhraj. Charles Sobhraj's birth name was Hatchand Bhaonani Gurumukh Charles Sobrhaj. Born on April 6th, 1944 in Saigon, Vietnam, his mother was Vietnamese and his father was an Indian Sindhi. Unfortunately for Sobhraj, he was born into an unhappy family, as his mother and father were unmarried. Soon after his birth, his father abandoned Sobhraj and his mother to fend for themselves. Even when he was adopted by his mother's new boyfriend, a French Army lieutenant stationed in Indochina, any hope of a pleasant childhood quickly died. Neglected by his mother and adopted father in favor of the couple's later children, Sobhraj was bounced back and forth between France and Indochina with the family. Sobhraj hated his life, and as a child he attempted, at least twice, to escape his circumstances to Saigon from France by sea, reaching as far as Djibouti on one occasion. As a teenager, Sobhraj found an outlet for his frustrations through committing petty crimes. In 1963, he would be caught and convicted of burglary, serving his first prison sentence at Poissy prison, located near Paris. Sobhraj quickly realized that his charisma could be used in his favor and began manipulating prison officials into granting him special privileges, such as being allowed to keep books in his cell, enjoy extra free time, etc. At around this same point in time, he met and gained the favor of Felix d'Escogne, a wealthy young man and frequent prison volunteer.

Almost immediately after being paroled, Sobhraj moved in with d'Escogne and began sharing his time between moving in the high societal circles of Paris and the criminal underworld. Through a series of scams and burglaries, Sobhraj began amassing an impressive fortune. During this lucrative time, he met and began a passionate relationship with Chantal Compagnon, a young Parisian woman from a conservative family. Sobhraj asked for Compagnon's hand in marriage, but any happiness would be abruptly cut short as he was arrested the very same day for evading police while driving a stolen car. Compagnon remained supportive through his conviction and subsequent eight month prison sentence, however, and the two were married soon after his release.

In 1970 Sobhraj and then pregnant Chantal fled France for Asia and a new life, far from French jurisdiction. As they traveled through Eastern Europe with forged travel documents, the two robbed tourists whom they befriended along the way to keep their cash flow and opulent lifestyle moving smoothly. Eventually, the Sobhrajs arrived in Mumbai where Chantal gave birth to a baby girl, named Usha. In the meantime, Sobhraj happily reestablished his criminal lifestyle, running a car theft and smuggling operation. Money needed to be quickly gathered to fuel his blossoming gambling addiction.

His system worked well for a few years until he was arrested and imprisoned in 1973 for an unsuccessful armed robbery attempt on a jewelry store at Hotel Ashoka. Soon after, Sobhraj managed to escape with some help from his wife after faking an illness. Freedom was short lived, however, because they were quickly re-captured and returned to jail. This time, Sobhraj borrowed money for bail from his father and fled, taking his family to Kabul.

The family never slowed down, continuing their hobby of robbing tourists on what was called the "Hippie Trail", but they were eventually arrested once again. Not long after Sobhraj escaped a second time, even using the same method he had implemented in India: faking illness and drugging the hospital guard. This time around, Sobhraj fled to Iran, leaving his family behind to fend for themselves. Chantal, though still fiercely loyal to Sobhraj, returned to France and vowed to never see her husband again. After all the arrests, scams, and turmoil, Chantal had grown tired of a criminal lifestyle and sought to build a better life for herself and her young daughter.

Sobhraj spent the next two years on the run, using as many as ten stolen passports. Over time, Sobhraj passed through various countries in Eastern Europe and the Middle East, and he was eventually joined by his younger brother, Andre, in Istanbul. The two brothers quickly became partners in crime, committing crimes throughout both Turkey and Greece. The pair were eventually apprehended in Athens, but an escape plan that involved an identity switch failed, leading to the escape of only one brother, Sobhraj. Andre was eventually turned over to the Turkish police by Greek authorities and served his eighteen year sentence alone.

Forever on the run from the law, Sobhraj financed his opulent lifestyle by posing as both a gem salesman and drug dealer to impress and befriend tourists, whom he would then defraud. His travels took him to Thailand, where Sobhraj met Marie-Andree Leclerc from Levis, Quebec. Leclerc was a young tourist looking for adventure, and she mistakenly believed she had found it in the charismatic company of Sobhraj. Charmed by Sobhraj's magnetic personality, Leclerc quickly became a loyal follower, looking the other way when he committed crimes and ignoring his philandering ways with the local women.

Sobhraj soon began collecting more and more followers by winning their loyalty. He did this most often by helping his targets out of difficult situations. In one instance he helped two former French policemen, Yannick and Jacques, recover their missing passports. Unbeknownst to the two men, Sobhraj had in fact stolen their original passports. Another scheme had Sobhraj providing shelter to a Frenchman, named Domnique Rennelleau, who seemed to be suffering from an intense case of dysentery. The terrible truth was that Sobhraj had actually been poisoning Rennelleau. Finally, he was joined by a young Indian, named Ajay Chowdhury. Also a long practiced criminal, Chowdhury became Sobhraj's second-in-command, dutifully following Sobhraj's every grizzly order.

Sobhraj and Chowdhury's first recorded murders occurred in 1975. It was in the city of Pattaya, Thailand that this serial killer's story truly began. On a usual early morning, a fisherman in a long boat found the body of a young woman, known today to be Teresa Knowlton of Seattle, floating in the water. When the royal Thai police were alerted, they rushed to the scene. The coroner examined the victim and questioned the fishermen, but there was little to go on. They found no identification, and there were no signs of foul play. The coroner could only conclude that the woman was most likely a young Western tourist whose vacation had come to an abrupt and tragic end by a terrible swimming accident. At the morgue, the coroner routinely took down her fingerprints, and the woman's identity was listed as "unknown". A toxicology report revealed alcohol and hashish in her system, and the medical examiner had seen enough cases like this in his career to believe this was little more than a case of an unsuspecting tourist deciding to take a late night swim and falling prey to the water's dangerous rip tides, confirming the initial police report. Police then went about the routine business of uncovering the woman's identity, canvassing hotels near where her body was found, but they found nothing. While the investigation was under way, the police waited for a missing person report to fall across their desk, hoping to find the drowning victim's identity this way. For two months, nothing happened, until another discovery grabbed the attention of the Royal Thai police.

A worker driving his truck near the very same beach noticed something unusual in the brush that lined the road. It was the body of a second young Westerner. Police immediately combed the area, but they found few clues. She was a young woman, perhaps a student on an overseas vacation, but there was no identification with her body. There was no purse, wallet, or even a passport. In the beginning, there was little to no alarm raised over this. Reporter Alan Dawson covered the two deaths.

"People didn't really correlate for a while the appearance of one body and then another," said Dawson.

One person that did choose to pay attention was Somphol Suthimai, a lieutenant colonel in the Thai police department who was also the head of Interpol in Thailand. It was not the similarities between the cases that caught Suthimai's attention, but the differences.

"They were both found near the seaside, but the condition that the bodies were in was different," said Suthimai.

The police report stated that the second woman was deliberately drowned, and this conclusion cast an ominous shadow over the first victim's case. Perhaps she had been deliberately drowned as well.

"Thai officials have a problem. They have [two] dead bodies. They have no identification associated with them. They know they have an investigation that they have to pursue criminally, but one of the key steps to getting it started is the identification of the victims," said John Imhoff, director of Interpol's US office at the time.

To help identify the two women, pictures of the victims were released to the Bangkok Post. Tens of thousands in Southeast Asia started their day by reading this English-language newspaper, and police hoped that one of these readers could help them acquire a lead. Days later, however, the two women remained unidentified. Pattaya, Thailand, was hardly the place one would expect a killing spree. Known as the Riviera of Thailand, Pattaya catered to Westerners; young men and women looking for a good time in an exotic land.

"Young people were attracted to Thailand. They thought that it had so much to offer compared with their culture, and they would soak it all up. This would make them especially vulnerable to the predators who were on the Hippy Trail," said Dawson.

Less than a month after the two women were found in Pattaya, villagers found two more bodies. This time, it was a man and a woman. They were clearly young and again Western, and they were very clearly murdered.

"The bodies were still burning when they were discovered. This was a horrific crime," remarked Dawson.

Both victim's faces were badly burned, and police looked for anything that could help them identify the pair or give them some sort of lead to go on. All they were able to find was a tag on the woman's clothing that read "Made in Holland". The police still had no leads and no motive, and using forensic evidence, they reconstructed the murders.

"The woman was beaten with a hard object. The man was whipped, strangled, until he couldn't breathe," recounted Suthimai.

The coroner also found soot in both of the victim's air passages, indicating that the pair was still alive when they are set on fire. The Thai police searched everywhere for suspects and leads, but their efforts turned up nothing. Three women and one man, all between the ages of 18 and 25, were dead. Police hoped that information would come in along the tourist trail and prayed that somewhere someone had come across the murdered foreigners and picked up information that might result in a lead.

Meanwhile, news had yet to reach Katmandu, Nepal, which lies at the end of the Hippy Trail nearly 1400 miles away. At the time, both Nepal and Thailand had only recently joined Interpol, and their communication was rudimentary at best. Officials here had no idea a killer was on the move until two bodies were discovered outside of Katmandu. A pair of Nepalese boys stumbled across the grizzly scene, and it was a sight they would never forget, nor would the investigators. It was difficult to identify who the victims were, as the woman had a wound on her chest, and the man had a wound on his neck. Nepalese detective Bishwa Lal Shrestha was the lead detective for the case.

"When we saw the dead bodies, the faces were burned. They were naked. We had no idea who could have done this," said Shrestha.

Police turned the boys that had found the victims away after securing the crime scene. Such a gruesome image was not for young eyes. Police suspected the couple were traveling together, and in Katmandu there is one place they were sure to have gone: Jhhonchen Tole, also known as "Freak Street". Investigators began their search there in the hotels and hostels that catered to tourists. At one such establishment, the host remembered a couple that had gone backpacking and had not returned for several days. Their names were , Henk Bintanja, 29, and his fiancée Cornelia Hemker, 25. When police searched their room, they found most of their belongings still there, but their passports were gone. They also found a diary, and written inside was the name Alain Gautier, from Bangkok, Thailand. Friends of the pair that were staying next door told police everything they knew about the couple's last known activities. They claimed they remembered seeing Hemker with a man who claimed to be a gem dealer from Bangkok. Police asked the friends to identify the bodies, and they confirmed that the bodies belonged to their missing friends.

Six bodies had now been found, but the two police departments still were not in communication. It was up to Interpol to apprehend this serial killer. So far, police had no idea that they were chasing the same man: Charles Sobhraj.

"Charles can present a persona that is what the people want to see, not what he really is, so if he wants to assume a false identity he's practiced this for a long time," remarked Imhoff.

The woman killed in Nepal had been seen with a gem dealer named Allan Gautier, an alias used by Sobhraj. Throughout Katmandu, officers continued to search for leads. At one hotel they found a clerk who remembered a guest matching Sobhraj's description, but he was not registered under Allan Gautier. He was registered as a Dutch national by the name of Karl Gassel. The clerk informed police that Gassel drove a white car. Is was not much of a lead, but police searched all the same, setting up check points and checking dozens of cars. An officer pulled over a vehicle that matched the description, and the driver was calm as he produced passports, identifying himself as Karl Gassel. The woman, his wife, was Ida Bosch. Police called off the search and escorted the couple to the station for questioning. The man claimed to be a scholar and his wife a Dutch television star. He insisted he had never seen the victim before. When the witness was brought in to identify him, she could not positively identify him as the same man she saw with her friend.

The police let the couple go. The man they knew as Karl Gassel and his wife returned to their hotel. Days later, a Katmandu policeman took a statement from a witness who saw a white car near where the bodies were found. Somehow, she even remembered the license plate number, which matched the plate on Gassel's car. Then came the hard evidence. Police found two arrival cards for the victim Pierre Beaumont, and the two signatures did not match. A handwriting expert found that aspects of the second signature were very similar to those of Gassel's. The second arrival card was also dated December the 24th, the same day Pierre Beaumont's corpse was brought in to the coroner's office. Police concluded that the man called Karl Gassel had left the country and returned using the dead man's passport. Now with a case against Gassel, police hurried to make an arrest. It was too late. Sobhraj and his companion were long gone. There were clothes, documents, tools for amending passports, and gasoline were found in the couple's apartment. It would be months before the information of Sobhraj and his escape reached Interpol.

"You can wait two days to get a call through to Nepal, and communications are not what they are now at all. By the time authorities could really make a case it was quite some time down the road and he was long gone," said Dawson.

In Thailand, there were still no suspects, and no identities for the four murdered Western tourists. They still had no idea that there are two additional victims in Nepal. Nothing like this had happened before, and police were investigating the possibility that the perpetrator was a Thai resident. While Thai police were hard at work, the Dutch embassy in Bangkok received a vital clue. Herman Knippenberg, a diplomat there, received a letter about a missing Dutch couple that had been vacationing in Thailand.

"I was very worried about the fact that for a period of over six weeks they had not had a sign of life from the couple," said Knippenberg.

Knippenberg had no idea at the time how important the couple's names would become. The names were Karl Gassel and Ida Bosch. In the missing couple's last letter they wrote that they had made a sophisticated new friend in Bangkok. The man was a gem dealer, and he was helping the pair buy and sell precious stones. The man had taken them to dinner and invited them to his apartment for drinks. That letter would be the last any of their families heard of their loved ones, Karl and Ida. Desperate and unable to help with their own power, family members asked Interpol's office in Thailand to help find their missing love ones. Knippenberg contacted Thai authorities and gave them the names of the two missing tourists, but the Thai police had no information about the missing couple. By communicating with the Australian office, Knippenberg learned of an Australian couple that were drugged and robbed by a gem dealer. This gem dealer ran by the name Alain Gautier. Sobhraj is a man capable of casting false lead after false lead, using his aliases to throw Interpol and local police off his trail for as long as he needs. By the time authorities discovered one of his aliases, he was long gone again, leaving victims dead or robbed in his wake. Such was the case with Alain Gautier the gem dealer.

Sobhraj's next victim was a nomadic Sephardic Jew by the name of Vitali Hakim, whose body was found on the side of a road leading to the Pattaya resort, where Sobhraj and his growing group of followers were staying. The young man's body was found with his neck snapped and partially burned with gasoline. Two Dutch students, Henk Bintanja, 29, and his fiancée Cornelia Hemker, 25, were invited to Thailand after meeting Sobhraj in Hong Kong. Following his usual scam, Sobhraj poisoned the young couple before nurturing them back to health and gaining their blind loyalty. As the pair were recovering, Sobhraj had a surprise visitor: the French girlfriend of Vitali Hakim, Charmayne Carrou, who had come demanding answers about her lover's sudden disappearance. Fearful of being exposed, Sobhraj and his murderous partner Chowdhury quickly moved to deal with the Dutch students that had heard too much. On December 16th, 1975, their damaged bodies were found strangled and burned. Soon after, poor Carrou was found drowned and wearing a bikini that was eerily similar to that which Teresa Knowlton had been found wearing. It would be months of fruitless searching and investigating before either women would be identified. It would be even longer before the two murders were connected, but Sobhraj would eventually be given the ominous nickname, "Bikini Killer".

On December 18th, the day the burned bodies of Bintanja and Hemker were identified, Sobhraj and Leclerc entered Nepal using the murdered pair's passports. After meeting in up inside the country on what investigators believe was either the 21st or 22nd of December, Sobhraj and Leclerc murdered Laurent Carriere, a 26-year-old from Canada, and Connie Bronzich, a 29-year-old from the United States. Some sources misidentified the pair as Laddie DuParr and Annabella Tremont. After their deaths, Sobhraj and Leclerc returned to Thailand, using Bintanja and Hemker's stolen passports before authorities could put anyone on alert for the missing documents. Upon his return, Sobhraj realized that his three French followers had begun to suspect him of his murders, having discovered his hidden stash of stolen documents belonging to the murder victims. The three notified authorities and fled for their lives back to Paris, convinced that Sobhraj would move to kill them for knowing too much.

Sobhraj next found himself in Calcutta, on the run as usual, where he killed Israeli professor Avoni Jacob. Investigators believe that Sobhraj committed the murder simply to acquire the victim's passport. Sobhraj used the stolen document to travel with Leclerc and Chowdhury. The small group hopped from Singapore, to India, and finally, back to Bangkok in March of 1976. They were quickly caught and given lengthy interrogations by Thai policemen regarding their possible connection to the murders, but they were eventually released because authorities feared the negative publicity that a murder trial would bring might harm the country's tourist industry.

At the same time, Dutch official Herman Knippenberg was still hot on the trail, investigating into the murders of Bintanja and Hemker. Knippenberg knew a little of, and had allegedly even met, Sobhraj, but his real name had not been obtained at that time and Sobhraj managed to slip out of Knippenberg's fingers. Knippenberg tirelessly gathered evidence, and, with the cooperation of Sobhraj's neighbor, slowly but surely built a case against him. Knippenberg eventually won permission from police to search Sobhraj's apartment, but this search did not occur until a full month after Sobhraj had left the country. In spite of this, Knippenberg was able to obtain a substantial amount of evidence, ranging from Sobhraj's victim's stolen documents and passports to poisons and syringes. Meanwhile, the three serial criminals stopped in Malaysia, where Chowdhury was sent to steal gems for a gem salesman scam. Chowdhury was seen delivering the gems to Sobhraj, but this would prove to be the last time Sobhraj's longtime partner would be seen alive. Neither Chowdhury nor his remains were ever found, and it is believed by investigators that Sobhraj murdered his former partner before leaving Malaysia. Leclerc and Sobhraj then moved to Geneva in order to sell the stolen gems as gem salesmen. Although Chowdhury was allegedly spotted in Germany, the claim has gone unsubstantiated, and the search for Chowdhury, alive or dead, continues.

Soon after returning to Asia, Sobhraj started to rebuild a new "family" of devoted followers, starting with two lost Western women, Barbara Smith and Mary Ellen Eather, in Bombay. Sobhraj's next believed victim was a Frenchman by the name of Jean-Luc Solomon, who he accidentally killed with poison. It is believed that in this case, Sobhraj intended merely to incapacitate the man so that he could be robbed. Sometime in July of 1976, Sobhraj, joined in New Delhi by his three female companions in crime, tricked a tour group of French post-graduate students into accepting them as tour guides. Sobhraj drugged the group, giving them poison laced pills that he told them were anti-dysentery medicine. The drugs acted more quickly than Sobhraj had estimated, however, and the students began losing consciousness. Seeing their comrades fall victim to the pills, the few that remained conscious realized what Sobhraj had done, overpowered him, and contacted police. This brave act finally lead to this career criminal and serial murderer's capture. Barbara and Mary Ellen quickly broke during interrogation and confessed to their involvement with

Sobhraj and his long list of crimes. Sobhraj was charged with the murder of Solomon, and all four were sent to Tihar prison, New Delhi, where they awaited trial. To Sobhraj, however, this was an experience he had had many times.

Barbara and Mary Ellen could not bear to face the consequences of their actions, and in the two years leading up to their trial each attempted suicide. On the other hand, an always prepared Sobhraj had smuggled precious gems into prison by hiding them within his body, and he immediately began bribing guards in order to live comfortably within the jail. Sobhraj quickly turned his trial into a one man show, hiring and firing lawyers without hesitation, bringing in his newly paroled brother Andre to assist, and even going so far as to go on a hunger strike. Although he was expected to receive the death penalty, a shocking conviction gave him only twelve years. It would seem this charismatic psychopath could not be touched. Leclerc was found guilty of the drugging of the French students, was eventually paroled, and returned to Canada. Her crime spree stopped there, as she developed ovarian cancer. She swore her innocence and remained dutifully loyal to Sobhraj until the day she died in her home in April of 1984.

Meanwhile, Sobhraj's constant bribery of prison guards at Tihar prison had reached incredible levels. He led a life of opulence and luxury within the jail, with his own TV and frequent gourmet food. His gregarious and persuasive personality had earned him key friendships with guards and fellow prisoners. His arrogance did not stop there, as he routinely gave interviews to Western authors and journalists, such as Oz magazine's Richard Neville in the late 1970s and Alan Dawson in 1984. He happily talked about his murders while never openly admitting to them, and he pretended that his choices were fueled by a hatred for Western imperialism in Asia. Sometime after Neville's book *The Life and Crimes of Charles Sobhraj* came out, a work based entirely on an extended taped conversation Sobhraj had with Neville, Sobhraj denied everything he had said to the reporter.

Even with all his built up luxuries, Sobhraj had a problem facing him at the end of his twelve year sentence. The arrest warrant he had acquired in Thailand would still be valid, meaning he would be extracted to Thailand and almost certainly executed. To avoid this inevitable doom, in March of 1986, Sobhraj threw an enormous party for his guards and fellow inmates, drugged them with large doses of sleeping pills, and simply walked out of jail after serving ten of his twelve years. It would not be long before inspector Madhukar Zende of the Mumbai police found and recaptured Sobhraj in O'Coquero Restaurant in Goa. His prison term was immediately increased by an additional ten years for his escape, but this was exactly what Sobhraj had hoped for. On the 17th of February, 1997, a 52-year-old Sobhraj was released with almost all of his warrants, case evidence, and even witnesses that would have put him away long lost or invalid. Without a country to extradite the murderer to, Indian authorities had no choice but to allow him to return to France.

Late into 2007, it was reported that Sobhraj's lawyer had appealed to the current French president, Nicolas Sarkozy, for intervention with Nepal. By 2008, Sobhraj had announced his new engagement to a Nepali woman by the name of Nihita Diswas. On the 7th of July, 2008, Sobhraj issued a press released through his fiancée Nihita, claiming that since he was never convicted of murder by a jury, the media should stop referring to him as a serial killer. It sparked a lot of controversy, and once again his face was plastered on news channels across the world.

Some believed that he married his fiancée on October 9th, 2008, while in jail on Bada Dashami, a Nepalese festival, but the claims were dismissed by jail authorities the following day. They did confirm, however, that Nihita and her family were allowed into the prison to conduct a tika ceremony along with the relatives of hundreds of other prisoners. They insisted that this was not a wedding at all but just a part of the ongoing Dashain festival, where elders place the vermilion mark on the foreheads of those younger than them to signify their blessings.

In July of 2010, The Supreme Court of Nepal delayed the verdict on an appeal served by Sobhraj against a district court's judgment which sent him to life in prison for the killing of American tourist Connie Bronzich in 1975. Sobhraj had appealed against the verdict in 2006, claiming that the verdict had been an unfair act of racism from the judges. On July 30th, 2010, the Nepalese Supreme Court moved to uphold the verdict issued by the district court, adding an additional year and a 2000Rs fine for using a fake passport to travel. The court further mandated the immediate seizure of all his properties. His mother-in-law, who was also his lawyer, Shakuntala Thapa, and his "wife" Nihita expressed unhappiness with the verdict, and Thapa claimed that Sobhraj had been denied justice and that the judiciary was corrupt. The two were detained and sent into judicial custody for contempt of court because of these opinionated remarks. Sobhraj may never have been caught in Nepal at all, had it not been for a journalist who happened to recognize him in Katmandu in 2003. It was this twist of fate that had him arrested for his murder of Bronzich and Carriere decades before. When arrested, it is reported that he denied ever having been to Nepal before and that he was there to make a TV documentary.

Sobhraj is currently awaiting another trial for a case against him in the Bhaktapur district court for the murder of Canadian tourist Laurent Carriere. As of September 2014, Sobraj was convicted in Nepal of another murder.

TED BUNDY

KENNETH PUTNAM

Ted Bundy is one of the most prolific serial killers of the 20th century, having kidnapped, raped, and murdered at least 36 attractive young women between 1973 and 1978 in Colorado, Oregon, Utah, Florida, and Washington; however, many assert that this figure could be much higher. He had also kept some of his victims' body parts—including heads—as trophies in a utility shed behind his Utah home, as well having engaged in necrophilia with decomposing corpses which he would groom and apply makeup.

A master manipulator and classic antisocial personality, Bundy escaped custody twice; once from court during his first murder trial and the second time from the Garfield County Jail in Colorado by sawing a hole in his cell ceiling. He was placed on the FBI's Ten Most Wanted list and was later arrested in Florida in February 1978 after stealing a car. He was sentenced to death in 1979 for the murder of two Florida State University sorority sisters, and again in 1980 for another murder.

Very charismatic and handsome, Bundy exploited these characteristics heavily with his young female victims in an effort to earn their sympathy trust. He would often approach potential victims in public places, feigning injury or impersonating an authority figure before overpowering them—usually by hitting them in the head with a crowbar—taking them to secluded locations, and raping and murdering them. Sometimes he would simply break into young women's homes and bludgeon them while they slept.

Bundy was originally incarcerated for aggravated kidnapping and attempted assault in 1975 in Utah; however, his list of homicide victims continued to grow. He escaped from custody twice in Colorado and subsequently committed three more murders before finally being apprehended in Florida in 1978. Ted Bundy was sentenced to death and was executed in the electric chair at Raiford Prison in Starke, Florida, on 24 January 1989.

Early Life

Theodore Robert Bundy—originally Theodore Robert Cowell—was born on 24 November 1946 at the Elizabeth Lund Home for Unwed Mothers in Burlington, Vermont. The social stigma of being a single mother was great at that time so Bundy's mother, Louise Cowell, took her infant son to live with her parents—Samuel and Eleanor—in Philadelphia where young Ted took on the Cowell surname and was told that they were, in fact, his parents and that his mother was his sister. Eventually, Bundy discovered the truth and harbored lifelong resentment toward his mother for lying to him.

Bundy's paternity has never been definitively proven. His birth certificate lists his father as Lloyd Marshall, an Air Force veteran and salesman; however, Louise has claimed that she was "seduced by 'a sailor'" whose name "may have been Jack Worthington" but nobody by that name was ever found in Navy or merchant marines records. Compounding the problem is that Bundy's grandfather, Samuel Cowell, has been rumored to be his biological father; thus making Bundy the product of incest; however, again, there is no evidence of this.

In interviews, Bundy spoke highly of his grandparents, especially expressing a fondness for his grandfather even though other family members described Samuel as a tyrannical bully and bigot who beat his wife and dog, abused his daughters, harmed neighborhood cats, and would sometimes "speak aloud to unseen presences". Bundy's grandmother was timid and obedient and was treated for her depression with electroconvulsive therapy.

Bundy exhibited disturbing behavior from a young age. At the age of three, he was alleged to have surrounded his sleeping aunt, Julia, with household knives—blades pointed toward her—and smiled at her when she had awakened.

In 1950, when Bundy was only four, Louise changed both her and her son's surname to Nelson and moved them both to Tacoma, Washington, to live with cousins Jane and Alan Scott. In 1951, Louise met hospital cook Johnny Culpepper Bundy at a church singles night and they married later that year. Johnny formally adopted young Ted and he adopted the last name of Bundy. Even with efforts to include young Ted in family activities along with his four half-siblings—who he was often left to babysit—he always was distant. Later, Bundy would tell his girlfriend that Johnny wasn't his real dad, wasn't smart enough, and didn't make much money.

Bundy confessed that he "chose to be alone" as an adolescent and neither had any natural inclination to develop any close friendships nor knew what drove people to be friends in the first place. He would later say that he "hit a wall" and his inability to comprehend social behavior stunted his social development, rendering him required to adopt a façade of social activity. He was terribly shy, self-doubting, and uncomfortable in social situations and often teased for being different. Despite this, he was a good student at Woodrow Wilson High School, was active in a local Methodist church, and was even involved with a local Boy Scout troop.

Bundy would also admit—while on death row—that a part of him as a young child was "fascinated by images of sex and violence" and he called this part "the entity". He enjoyed reading crime books and detective magazines, particularly those that contained descriptions of sexual violence and pictures of dead bodies. Later, before his execution, he would admit that pornography was central in shaping who he was.

Throughout high school Bundy loved to ski and was very good at it; however, his pursuit of this hobby was usually accomplished with stolen equipment and forged lift tickets. He was also arrested on at least two occasions on suspicion of auto theft and burglary but when he turned 18 his juvenile record was expunged. Stealing, for Bundy, did not involve any guilt and, in fact, he had a sense of entitlement about the entire thing. He often said that the thrill of taking possession of something he wanted without remorse was exciting. Many speculate that his "taking" of his victims represented this same concept and provided him with the same rush. Compounding the problem was his sense of entitlement and cunning ability to lie about everything which demonstrates a common trait among psychopaths.

Bundy graduated high school in 1965 and was awarded a scholarship by the University of Puget Sound where he started that fall, taking courses in Oriental studies and psychology. After two semesters he transferred to the University of Washington in Seattle.

He obtained employment as a stock boy and bagger at a Safeway store on Queen Anne Hill, in addition to other odd jobs. As part of his psychology curricula, he would work as a night-shift volunteer at Seattle's Suicide Hot Line where he met and worked Ann Rule who would later become among the world's foremost true crime writers and who penned a biography about Bundy—that was also partly autobiographical about her working relationship with him—entitled *The Stranger Beside Me* (1980).

While in college, circa 1968, Bundy began a relationship with fellow student "Stephanie Brooks" (a pseudonym); however, after she graduated in 1968 and prepared to move back home to California she broke up with Bundy due to what she described as his lack of ambition and immaturity. Bundy was heartbroken after this and, interestingly, all of his victims bore some resemblance to Brooks; particularly the fact that Brooks and all of his victims had long dark hair which they wore parted down the middle.

Shortly thereafter, Bundy returned to Burlington—his birthplace—and learned the truth of his parentage. This discovery made him more dominant and focused.

He managed the Seattle office of Nelson Rockefeller's presidential campaign in 1968 and attended the 1968 Republican convention in Miami, Florida. He reenrolled at the University of Washington with a major in psychology. He became popular among his professors as he was an honor student and also began a relationship with Elizabeth Kloepfer in 1969. Kloepfer was a divorced secretary with a young daughter and the two dated for the next six years until he went to prison in 1976.

Bundy graduated in 1972 with a degree in psychology and went to work for the state Republican Party.

In the fall of 1973, Bundy enrolled in the University of Utah Law School but did poorly because of poor attendance and, consequently, dropped out the following spring.

While in California on a business trip in the summer of 1973, Bundy found his ex-girlfriend "Stephanie Brooks" and the change in his look and attitude was appealing to her. Bundy courted Brooks the rest of the year—while still involved with Kloepfer—and proposed to her, only to dump Brooks shortly after the new year, likely in retaliation for her breaking his heart years earlier. The breakup wreaked havoc on Bundy who became obsessed with her and this obsession "would span his lifetime and lead to a series of events that would shock the world".

Mere weeks later, Bundy began his first murderous rampage in Washington; however, many Bundy experts assert that he likely starting killing in his teens. One case involved eight-year-old Ann Marie Burr from Tacoma who disappeared from her home in 1961 when Bundy was 14. Burr's house was on Bundy's newspaper delivery route and her father was positive that he saw Bundy near a construction site ditch on the nearby University of Puget Sound campus the day his daughter vanished. Despite other potentially incriminating circumstantial evidence, Bundy remains merely a suspect due to a lack of consensus by law enforcement personnel as to whether they believe he actually did it or not. Bundy has always denied killing her.

Shortly before his execution, Bundy did, in fact, tell his attorney that his first attempt at kidnapping was in 1969 and his first "actual murder" occurred "sometime in 1972". While he was a suspect in the December 1973 murder of Kathy Devine in Washington, DNA analysis exonerated him and her true murderer was convicted in 2002.

Bundy's earliest identified murders were committed in 1974 when he was 27.

Bundy was a handsome and charismatic guy, particularly to his young female victims and he exploited these characteristics fully. He was also an adept chameleon, able to blend in and feign belonging which increased his threat to the attractive brunette women he targeted as his victims. This charm and his adroitness at lying and manipulation made him extremely dangerous.

Known Murder Victims

Karen Sparks (often referred to as Joni Lenz), 18 (survived)

On 4 January 1974, 18-year-old Karen Sparks/Joni Lenz was found by her roommates when she didn't emerge from her bedroom that morning. They were not prepared for what horrific sights they saw. Sparks had been beaten badly and a bed rod ripped from the bed was "savagely rammed into her vagina". Sparks was transported to the hospital in a coma and suffered damages which continue to plague her.

However, she was one of the lucky few victims to survive an attack by Bundy.

Lynda Ann Healy, 21

A very accomplished and beautiful young woman, 21-year-old Lynda Healy announced ski conditions for all of the western Washington resorts on the radio. A senior at the University of Washington, she came from a good family, loved to sing, and was majoring in psychology. She shared a house with four other young women near the university. On 31 January, Healy and some friends went to a tavern and then home to bed. Her roommate in the next room never heard any sounds emanating from Healy's room that night.

The following morning when she didn't emerge from her bedroom after her alarm clock sounded at its usual 5:30 a.m. to go to work—and her job called looking for her—her roommate noticed that her bed was made in a peculiar way. Further inspection showed that the top sheet and a pillowcase were missing, a small bloodstain that was the same type as Lynda's was on the pillow and the bottom sheet, and a bloody nightgown was hanging in her closet. One of her outfits was missing. Also worrisome was that one of the doors was unlocked.

Initially, due to the absence of fingerprint, hair, or fiber evidence, police did not suspect foul play; however, later, they did come to realize that an intruder came in, removed Healy's nightgown and dressed her in another outfit, made the bed, wrapped her up, and took her out of the house.

Donna Gail Manson, 19

On 12 March, in Olympia, 19-year-old Evergreen State College student Donna Manson was kidnapped and murdered.

Susan Elaine Rancourt, 18

On 17 April, Susan Rancourt, 18, disappeared from the Central Washington State College campus in Ellensburg while walking across campus, alone, at night.

Later, two other female coeds would report meeting a good-looking man with his arm in a cast—one the night Rancourt disappeared and one three nights earlier—who asked for assistance with carrying books to his VW Beetle.

Roberta Kathleen "Kathy" Parks, 22

Kathy Parks, 22, was last seen on 6 May on the Oregon State University campus in Corvallis en route to meeting friends for coffee.

Brenda Carol Ball, 22

22-year-old Brenda Ball was last seen leaving the Flame Tavern in Burien, Oregon on 1 June.

Georgeann Hawkins, 18

In the early morning hours of 11 June, University of Washington student and a member of Kappa Alpha Theta Georgeann Hawkins, 18, left her boyfriend's dormitory en route to her sorority house through an alley. She was never seen again; however, witnesses later stated they had seen a man with a leg cast struggling to carry a briefcase in that area. Another female coed reported that he had asked her for help in carrying his briefcase to his VW Beetle.

Bundy later confessed to having lured Hawkins to his car, clubbed her with a tire iron he had hidden underneath his vehicle, and then took her elsewhere to rape and strangle her to death.

Janice Ann Ott, 23, and Denise Marie Naslund, 19

On 14 July, Janet Ott, 23, and Denise Naslund, 19, were abducted mere hours apart from Lake Sammamish State Park in Issaquah, Washington, in broad daylight. On that day, eight different witnesses reported seeing a handsome young man with his arm in a sling who called himself "Ted" and who asked several women for help unloading a sailboat from his VW Beetle. One witness said she walked with him for a ways but didn't see a sailboat and then declined to help him. Other witnesses stated that they saw the man approach Ott and she was observed walking away with him.

Naslund disappeared four hours later.

At this point, police in King County put up fliers with the suspected murderer's description all over the Seattle area. One of Bundy's psychology professors, former coworker Ann Rule, and Bundy's girlfriend Elizabeth Kloepfer reported him as a possible suspect. In fact, Kloepfer (who since changed her surname to Kendall and penned a book called *The Phantom Prince: My Life with Ted Bundy* in 1981) told the Seattle Police Department that her boyfriend "might be involved" in the recent Seattle murders. She called again later that autumn with more information and agreed to give them recent pictures of Bundy to be shown to witnesses; however, many of them could not positively identify him.

Ott's and Naslund's remains were found on 7 September off Interstate 90 near Issaquah, only one mile from the park where they were abducted. Near the women's remains was an extra femur and vertebrae which Bundy confessed before his execution belonged to Hawkins.

Between 1 March and 3 March 1975, the skulls and jawbones belonging to Healy, Rancourt, Parks, and Ball were found just east of Issaquah on Taylor Mountain. Bundy confessed in his death row interview that he kept the decapitated heads of these four victims in his apartment for some time and that he would revisit this dump site often to engage in sex with the corpses until decomposition became too great to continue. Bundy also admitted that he dumped Manson's body there as well—but burned her skull in his girlfriend's fireplace—however, no trace of her was ever recovered.

Other trophies discovered when Bundy's apartment was searched include photographs of his victims and a large bag of women's clothing.

Nancy Wilcox, 16

Bundy began the University of Utah Law School in the autumn of 1974. On 2 October 1974, 16-year-old Nancy Wilcox disappeared from Holladay, Utah. She was last seen in a VW Beetle.

Melissa Smith, 17

On 18 October, 17-year-old Melissa Smith—the daughter of Midvale, Utah's Police Chief Louis Smith—disappeared after leaving a pizza parlor. Nine days later she was found strangled, raped, and sodomized.

Laura Aime, 17

17-year-old Laura Aime disappeared from a Halloween party in Lehi, Utah. Her naked corpse was found on Thanksgiving Day by hikers near a river in the Wasatch Mountains. She had been beaten about the head and face with a crowbar and was raped and sodomized. The lack of blood at the crime scene indicated that she was likely killed elsewhere and dumped in this location. Police found no other physical evidence.

Carol DaRonch, 18 (survived)

On 8 November, 18-year-old Carol DaRonch was shopping at the Fashion Place Mall in Salt Lake City, Utah, and was approached by a man in the Sears parking lot who claimed to be a police officer named Officer Roseland. He told her that her car had been stolen and that he would take her to the police station to retrieve it. He took her to his VW Beetle and she became suspicious and asked him for identification. He quickly flashed a gold badge and she got in but refused his order to fasten her seat belt. After a short distance, Bundy pulled over and attempted to place handcuffs on DaRonch but only managed one wrist. He also attempted to hit her with a crowbar which she was able to catch before it hit her head. DaRonch fought back, kicking him in the groin, and as the car was speeding away she jumped out of it.

DaRonch flagged down another car and they took her to the police who confirmed there was no Officer Roseland. Police were able to obtain a description of the assailant and his car and a blood sample from DaRonch's coat. Type O; the same as Bundy's.

Debra Kent, 17

Mere hours after losing DaRonch Bundy abducted 17-year-old Debra "Debi" Kent from the parking lot of a school in Bountiful, Utah, as she was leaving a school play. She had told her parents she was going to pick up her brother at the bowling alley and she would be back to pick them up soon but never returned. She didn't even make it to her car which was still in the parking lot. Police found a small handcuff key in the parking lot and when they tried the key in the handcuffs DaRonch was wearing, it was a perfect fit.

A month later a man called the police and told them that he saw a tan VW Beetle speeding away from the high school parking lot the night Kent disappeared.

Shortly before he was to be executed, Bundy confessed that he dumped Kent's body near Fairview, Utah. After an intense search of the area, a human kneecap which was consistent with someone of Kent's age and size was found; however, DNA analysis was not conducted.

Caryn Campbell, 23

Bundy's first murder of 1975 occurred on 12 January. 23-year-old Michigan nurse Caryn Campbell disappeared between her hotel's lounge and her room while on a ski trip with her fiancé, Dr. Raymond Gadowski, and his two children, in Snowmass, Colorado. Frantic Gadowski called the police the next morning but a search proved futile.

Nearly a month later—and only a few short miles from where she went missing—a recreational worker discovered Campbell's nude body near the road. Animal damage to her body made it difficult to determine the exact cause of death; however, there was evidence of repeated, crushing blows to her head by a sharp instrument. Some of the blows were so violent that one of her teeth separated from the gums.

Julie Cunningham, 26

On 15 March, 26-year-old Vail ski instructor Julie Cunningham disappeared on her way to a nearby tavern. Bundy confessed in prison that he used his crutches ploy to approach Cunningham to ask for her help carrying ski boots to his car before he clubbed her with his crowbar, handcuffed her, and took her to a secluded location where strangled her.

Denise Oliverson, 25

25-year-old Denise Oliverson vanished in Grand Junction on 6 April while riding her bicycle to visit her parents.

Lynette Culver, 13

13-year-old Lynette Culver was abducted from her school playground at Alameda Junior High School in Pocatello, Idaho.

Susan Curtis, 15

Once Bundy returned to Utah, 15-year-old Susan Curtis vanished on 28 June while walking alone to the Brigham Young University dormitories during a youth conference she was attending. Bundy confessed to her murder minutes before his execution.

The bodies of Cunningham, Oliverson, Culver, and Curtis have never been found.

First Arrest, Trial, and Escapes

Bundy was first arrested on 16 August 1975 in Salt Lake City for failure to stop his vehicle for police. A search of his car unearthed a crowbar, handcuffs, ski mask, trash bags, an icepick, and other items the officer thought were burglary tools. The always calm and collected Bundy explained reasons why he had the items such as that he used the mask for skiing and had found the handcuffs in a dumpster; however, Detective Jerry Thompson connected Bundy and his Volkswagen to the DaRonch kidnapping and other missing girls and searched his apartment.

The search yielded a brochure of Colorado ski resorts with a checkmark by where Campbell had disappeared. Bundy was brought in for a lineup before DaRonch and other witnesses at the time DaRonch was kidnapped and they all identified him as Officer Roseland, as well as the man lurking about on the night Debbie Kent vanished.

After a week-long trial, Bundy was convicted on 1 March 1976 of kidnapping DaRonch and was sentenced to 15 years in Utah State Prison. Bundy was then extradited to Colorado to stand trial for murder.

He was able to escape custody twice before his eventual final arrest in Florida. The first escape occurred on 7 June 1977, when he was transported from the Garfield County Jail in Glenwood Springs, Colorado, to Pitkin County Courthouse in Aspen for his preliminary hearing. As he was serving as his own attorney, the judge excused him from being handcuffed and shackled. During a recess Bundy asked if he could research his case in the courthouse's law library. Hiding behind a bookcase he jumped from a second-story window, spraining his ankle when he landed. After shedding his suit, he simply walked through the town of Aspen as roadblocks were being erected before hiking southward on Aspen Mountain.

Near its summit he burglarized a cabin and stole clothing, food, and a rifle before heading toward Crested Butte; however, Bundy became lost and ended up wandering aimlessly for two days before breaking into a camping trailer on Maroon Lake where he took more food and a parka. Bundy then walked back toward Aspen and stole a car parked at the Aspen Golf Course. Two police officers noticed him weaving in traffic and pulled over the six-day fugitive. In the car were maps of the mountains around Aspen that the prosecutor was using to demonstrate where victim Caryn Campbell's body was found. As Bundy was his own attorney, he had the right of discovery to this evidence, thus demonstrating that he had planned his escape.

Bundy's second escape occurred on 30 December 1977, after having his motion for a change of venue to Denver accepted but with the venue being Colorado Springs instead; a city that had historically been hostile to murder suspects. He had managed to acquire the jail's floor plan and a hacksaw blade from other inmates, as well as $500 in cash smuggled in over a six-month period by visitors—particularly one Carole Ann Boone. In the evening while other inmates were showering, Bundy sawed a one-foot-square hole in his cell's ceiling—behind the steel bars—and was able to fit through it into the crawlspace above after losing 35 pounds. Prior to his actual escape, Bundy "practiced" and multiple reports of possible movement in the ceiling's crawlspace were, curiously, never investigated.

On the night of his escape, Bundy piled files and books under his covers in his bunk to look like his sleeping body, climbed into the crawlspace, broke through the jail's ceiling which, incidentally, was the chief jailer's apartment who just happened to be out for the evening with his wife. Bundy stole some street clothes and casually sauntered out the front door.

Bundy stole a car and drove east; however, the car broke down on Colorado's Interstate 70. A passing motorist gave him a ride into Vail where he caught a bus to Denver and then took a flight to Chicago, Illinois. From there he took an Amtrak train to Ann Arbor, Michigan.

His escape was discovered over 17 hours after the fact at noon on New Year's Eve.

Lisa Levy, 20, Margaret Bowman, 21, Karen Chandler (survived), Kathy Kleiner Deshields (survived)

On 15 January 1978—after Bundy had escaped from jail in Colorado, he traveled to Tallahassee, Florida, and attacked Chi Omega sorority sisters at Florida State University. At approximately 3:00 a.m. he entered the sorority house where he raped and strangled 20-year-old Lisa Levy to death; bludgeoned 21-year-old Margaret Bowman to death; and also bludgeoned Karen Chandler and Kathy Kleiner—both of whom survived.

The entire rampage took only 30 minutes.

Cheryl Thomas (survived)

That same morning, a mere eight blocks from the Chi Omega sorority house, Bundy attacked Cheryl Thomas in her bed and bludgeoned her with a wooden club, severely injuring her.

Kimberly Leach, 12

On 9 February, Bundy kidnapped 12-year-old Kimberly Leach from her junior high school in Lake City, Florida. Her raped, murdered, and dumped body was found in Suwannee River State Park underneath a small pig shed.

Bundy then stole another VW Beetle and left Tallahassee, traveling west across the Florida panhandle.

Florida Arrest

On 15 February 1978 shortly after 1:00 a.m., Bundy was stopped by Pensacola police officer David Lee who learned that the vehicle was stolen. After a brief scuffle, Lee had subdued and restrained Bundy and then took him to jail. During the transport, Bundy allegedly told Lee that he wished the officer would have killed him. Once his identity was confirmed, Bundy was transported to Tallahassee and charged with the Tallahassee and Lake City murders.

Florida Trials and Convictions

Among the most damning evidence during Bundy's June 1979 Chi Omega murder trial were bite marks found on Lisa Levy's left buttock which matched a plaster cast taken from Bundy's mouth. Additionally, Chi Omega sister Nita Neary was returning home late that night and saw Bundy as he left. She was able to identify him in court.

Bundy was convicted on all counts and sentenced to death.

In 1980, Bundy stood trial for the Kimberly Leach murder. Again, he was convicted, this time based upon fiber evidence and an eyewitness who saw him leading Leach away from the school. Bundy was, again, sentenced to death.

After his sentences he sought a stay of execution or commutation of his death sentences to life imprisonment by having one of his legal advocates contact his victims' families to ask them to ask for mercy in order to find out where their loved ones' remains were. This ploy for more time failed.

Execution

Bundy ultimately met his demise in Raiford Prison's electric chair on 24 January 1989.

Shortly before his widely-publicized execution, Bundy confessed to 36 murders in seven states; however, many believe that the total number is much higher. Also before his execution, Bundy contacted Dr. James Dobson, psychologist and founder of the Christian evangelical organization Focus on the Family, and agreed to a television interview the day before his execution. In it, Bundy described the influence of pornography on his behavior. While not expressly blaming pornography for his behavior, Bundy did say that pornographic materials shaped and molded his behavior and he would gradually need more violent, graphic, and explicit material to achieve the same "high"; not unlike a drug addict. He claimed that while murdering he was "possessed by 'something ... awful and alien'" and the brutal urge was indescribable. He also claimed that alcohol helped remove the initial boundary for him to commit his first murder. Bundy also admitted that although he believed he deserved the death penalty, he didn't want to die.

Even today, Bundy remains a suspect in a number of open homicide cases and is likely responsible for other victims who will never be identified. In 1987 he confided to Keppel that there were some murders that he would "never talk about" because they were committed too close to home, involved victims who were very young, or were too close to family. Said victims include the aforementioned Ann Marie Burr who Bundy repeatedly denied having murdered; however, Keppel noticed that Burr fits all three of Bundy's "no discussion" categories. In 2011, forensic testing of material from the Burr crime scene did not have enough intact DNA sequences to compare to Bundy's.

Additional potential victims include flight attendants Lisa E. Wick and Lonnie Trumbull, both 20, who were bludgeoned with a piece of wood while asleep in their Seattle home on 23 June 1966 that was very near the Safeway store where Bundy worked at the time, and where the victims regularly shopped. Trumbull did not make it and Wick suffered permanent memory loss.

On 30 May 1969 college friends Susan Davis and Elizabeth Perry, both 19, who were on vacation in Atlantic City, New Jersey—just 60 miles south of Philadelphia—were found stabbed to death in the woods three days later.

On 19 July 1971, 24-year-old elementary school teacher and motel maid Rita Curran was murdered in her basement apartment in Burlington, Vermont. She had been bludgeoned, raped, and strangled. The motel where she worked part-time was adjacent to the Elizabeth Lund Home where Bundy was born and certain similarities to his other crime scenes made Bundy a suspect.

21-year-old Joyce LePage was last seen alive on 22 July 1971 on the Washington State University campus. Nine months later her skeleton was found wrapped in military blankets, carpeting, and rope, at the bottom of a Pullman, Washington, ravine.

On 29 June 1973, 17-year-old Rita Lorraine Jolly disappeared from West Linn, Oregon while 24-year-old Vicki Lynn Hollar disappeared from Eugene, Oregon, on 20 August of that same year. Bundy had confessed to two Oregon homicides but did not identify the victims.

Brenda Joy Baker, 14, was last seen hitchhiking near Puyallup, Washington on 27 May 1974 and her body would be discovered a month later in Millersylvania State Park.

19-year-old Wisconsin native Sandra Jean Weaver who had been living in Tooele, Utah, was last seen on 1 July 1974 in Salt Lake City. Her nude body was found the following day in Grand Junction, Colorado.

20-year-old Carol Valenzuela was last seen hitchhiking near Vancouver, Washington, on 2 August 1974 and her remains were found two months later in a shallow grave south of Olympia; along with the remains of another female who was later identified as 17-year-old Martha Morrison who was last seen in Eugene, Oregon, on 1 September 1974. During this time, Bundy drove from Seattle to Salt Lake City and could have conceivably passed through both towns; however, there is no definitive evidence.

Bundy is also a suspect in Melanie Suzanne Cooley's disappearance on 15 April 1975 after leaving Nederland High School in Nederland, Colorado. Her beaten and strangled corpse was discovered on 2 May by road maintenance workers nearby in Coal Creek Canyon. Whereas gas receipts place Bundy in Golden that day—not far from Nederland—the Jefferson County Sheriff's Office has classified her murder as a cold case.

On 1 July 1975, Shelly Kay Robertson, 24, failed to show up for work in Golden, Colorado, and her nude, decomposed corpse was found in August inside of a mine on Berthoud Pass near Winter Park. While gas station receipts place Bundy in the area, there is no direct evidence as to his complicity.

23-year-old Nancy Perry Baird disappeared from the Farmington, Utah, service station where she worked on 4 July 1975. She officially remains a missing person and Bundy has repeatedly denied involvement.

Finally, 17-year-old Debbie Smith was last seen in February 1976 in Salt Lake City before the DaRonch trial. Her body was found near the airport on 1 April 1976.

Aftermath

During the Kimberly Leach trial, Bundy married Carole Ann Boone. He took advantage of an existing Florida statute in which a marriage declaration in court in front of a judge constituted a legal marriage. Thus, Bundy called Boone as a character witness and married her while she was on the witness stand. After numerous conjugal visits, Boone gave birth to a daughter in October 1982. She returned to Washington in 1986 with her daughter after divorcing him and never returned.

Ann Rule described Bundy as "... a sadistic sociopath who took pleasure from another human's pain and the control he had over his victims, to the point of death, and even after." He once referred to himself as "the most cold-hearted son of a bitch you'll ever meet" and one of his defense attorneys, Polly Nelson, said that Bundy "was the very definition of heartless evil." At one point, Bundy said, "We serial killers are your sons, we are your husbands, we are everywhere. And there will be more of your children dead tomorrow."

Bundy contacted Robert Keppel—the detective who helped put him in prison—while on death row to assist him with the "Green River Killer" investigation at the time. With Bundy's assistance, Keppel was able to understand the inner workings of the mind of a serial killer and was, subsequently, able to identify and apprehend Gary Ridgway in November 2001.

Ted Bundy has been the subject of three television movies and one feature film. The two-part film entitled *The Deliberate Stranger* aired on NBC in 1986, starring Mark Harmon as Bundy. *Ted Bundy* (2002) starred Michael Reilly Burke as Bundy and was directed by Matthew Bright. In 2003 the USA Network aired Ann Rule's *The Stranger Beside Me* that starred Billy Campbell as Bundy and Barbara Hershey as Rule. Finally, the A&E network produced an adaptation of detective Robert Keppel's book *The Riverman* in 2004, starring Cary Elwes as Bundy and Bruce Greenwood as Keppel.

THE TRAILSIDE KILLER

JACK BENSTON

64

David Carpenter ("Trailside Killer")

David Carpenter, also known as the Trailside Killer, stalked, sexually assaulted, and murdered mostly women on hiking trails near San Francisco, California, with a few victims in Santa Cruz, California. Most of his victims were shot in the head, execution-style, while a couple of them were stabbed to death. Carpenter's reign of terror lasted from 1979 into 1981 when he was subsequently arrested, tried, and convicted of death.

One of his victims, Stephen Haertle, survived being shot multiple times by Carpenter—even though his girlfriend Ellen Hansen was killed—and was able to give police a description of his assailant. Additional witness testimony placed a small red foreign car in the area. Carpenter matched the composite drawn from Haertle's description and he also owned a car that matched the description of the one on the scene at the time of Hansen's and Haertle's attack.

Carpenter was convicted in two separate trials; one in Los Angeles and one in San Diego. Both trials were relocated due to defense attorneys' requests for changes of venue.

He was ultimately sentenced to death and is currently on San Quentin's death row. Carpenter is 85 years of age.

Early Life

David Joseph Carpenter was born on 6 May 1930 in San Francisco—a place that would later become his hunting grounds. As a child, he was physically abused and neglected by his alcoholic father while his near-blind mother was overly domineering. By the time he was seven years old, his stutter was so bad that he couldn't function in any social situation. Many experts assert that his stuttering was likely a result of stress, self-perceived inadequacy, and not feeling safe as a child. Consequently he was ridiculed which made him overly reclusive. Instead of therapy he was forced to take ballet and piano lessons.

To relieve his frustrations, Carpenter suffered from a bedwetting problem and also tortured animals; thus fulfilling two of the three prongs of the classic serial killer triad, with the other being a preoccupation with setting fires.

From a young age he also had an insatiable sex drive and would look for opportunities to express this. At the age of 17 Carpenter was incarcerated for molesting two of his young cousins. He served a year in the custody of the California Youth Authority and apparently learned nothing because after his release he was even more predatory; offending until he got married in 1955.

Carpenter worked a number of jobs, including as a cruise ship's purser, a salesman, and a printer.

Carpenter and his wife had three children and Carpenter's demanding libido got to be too much for her. Eventually his wife was not enough to satisfy him. In addition to his violent rages he would prowl around, looking for other women. When his drive became so desperate, he resorted to violence.

By serial killer standards, Carpenter was a late bloomer. His first serious violent offense occurred in 1960 when he was arrested and incarcerated for attempted murder for attacking a woman with a hammer and knife. He had befriended this woman and invited her over to meet his wife and family. One day he picked her up for work but instead of driving her there he drove to a wooded area near the Presidio and then pretended to be lost. At some point he grabbed her, straddled her, and tied her up with a clothesline. He then threatened her with a knife, forcing her to be still and telling her that he had a "funny quirk" that needed to be satisfied. When she resisted he struck her multiple times with a hammer. Her cries for help alerted a nearby military patrol officer who, essentially, saved her life. When commanded to stop, Carpenter shot at the officer and was met with return gunfire which wounded Carpenter. He was then arrested. The victim survived. The victim described his speech to investigators as slow and deliberate, thus suggesting that when Carpenter feels as though he is in charge of a situation and asserting himself then he loses his stutter.

While initially sentenced to 14 years, Carpenter served just nine before being released in 1969. Tired of his sexual demands and temper—and having just given birth to their third child—his wife divorced him. When questioned about what caused the divorce Carpenter's story would change, thus indicating that he learned to tell people what he thought they wanted to hear.

Carpenter was remarried quickly after his release and in less than a year this marriage failed as he was back to his old tricks. He once tried to rape a woman by hitting her car to force her out of it. As she struggled with him he stabbed her but she managed to get back into her car and get help.

At this point there is little doubt that Carpenter wanted to rape again but not return to prison so he was prepared to eliminate any witnesses.

He was rearrested on 3 February 1970, in Modesto, California, on kidnapping and robbery charges. Before being transferred to prison, however, he and four other inmates escaped from the Calaveras County Jail. After recapture by the Federal Bureau of Investigation, Carpenter was incarcerated for seven years on the kidnapping and robbery charges, with two more for violating parole. He served his time and was then paroled in May 1979, without being listed as a sex offender which he should have been. In August of that year he murdered his first of many victims.

Carpenter found a job at a photo print shop in San Francisco after he left prison and by all measures appeared to be on the right path to becoming a productive and law-abiding citizen.

The Crimes

Edda Kane

44-year-old married bank executive Edda Kane disappeared from Mount Tamalpais Park near San Francisco Bay on 19 August 1979, while hiking in the part of the park nicknamed "the Sleeping Lady" to revel in the glorious view of the Golden Gate Bridge. As she enjoyed an athletic lifestyle and could not find someone to accompany her on her hike that day, she decided to go out alone. When she did not return home that day her husband called the police who sent out a search team with dogs in case she had fallen and required assistance.

Kane's vehicle was in the parking lot where she left it but there were no signs of the missing woman.

She was later found off Rock Spring Trail on 20 August 1979, naked and shot to death. Forensic experts surmised that she had been attacked from behind and then shot execution-style with a bullet in the back of the head based upon the position of her body on its knees with her face in the dirt. $10 was missing from her wallet, along with some credit cards. The attacker took her glasses but left her jewelry.

This was the first murder on Mount Tamalpais.

Kane's autopsy demonstrated that she had been shot once in the back of the head with a .44 caliber gun. As she had not been raped, police were dumbfounded as to the motive for the attack. Nobody who knew the victim could think of anyone who would want to do her any harm and the lack of evidence did not permit police to fully investigate her death. After a short time her murder became an unsolved isolated homicide and things returned to normal until the following spring.

Barbara Schwartz

On 7 March 1980, 23-year-old baker Barbara Schwartz had gone hiking in Mount Tamalpais State Park with her dog and had never returned.

She was found on a narrow unpaved trail, stabbed to death in the chest. A witness who had watched the entire crime ran for help and, thus, led the rangers to the crime scene. The witness was hiking in the area when she saw through the trees a thin, athletic man, about 25 years of age approach Schwartz whose dog was barking. She said the assailant "had a hawk nose and dark hair, and he wore hiking boots." The witness then stated that the man and victim struggled for nearly a minute and then he left as Schwartz fell to the ground which was when she left to seek help. Unfortunately, the witness' description of the assailant was "wildly erroneous in every respect" and she, in fact, later admitted this herself. Consequently, investigators were misled, thus delaying the search for the actual culprit.

Other witnesses said they had seen a lone male in his 40s, wearing glasses, and clad in a raincoat despite the fact that it wasn't raining that day. This man was most likely Schwartz's killer.

The bifocals found near Schwartz's body turned out to be prison-issued so investigators began to look at recently-released convicts, particularly those with a record of sex crimes who bore some resemblance to the witness description of the assailant. The San Francisco office of the FBI assisted with the investigation but to no avail.

Interestingly, however, police in another jurisdiction did question a man who claimed to have been wounded in a convenience store attack; however, these officers did not have access to the Marin County all-points bulletin and, therefore, were unable to make a possible connection that this quiet man may have been responsible for Schwartz's murder. The next day the same wounded man visited an optometrist—Schwartz's doctor, in fact—to get a new pair of glasses. The previous day the police had questioned the doctor about Schwartz's prescription; however, he had no knowledge of the eyeglasses found at the scene of the crime. If he had then he might have recognized the "unique prescription" his new patient had.

During Schwartz's autopsy, the pathologist counted 12 separate stab wounds in her chest, likely made with a ten-inch knife. Several days later, some kids found a blood-crusted boning knife near the crime scene which was determined to have been purchased at a large chain grocery store. A television reporter had subsequently handled the knife, thus obliterating any fingerprints which might have been left by the murderer. Forensic evidence suggested that she, too, had been in a kneeling position when she died.

Anne Alderson

On 15 October 1980, 26-year-old former Peace Corps volunteer Anne Alderson entered the park to go for a jog and to demonstrate that the park was, for the most part, safe. Many witnesses saw her and the park's caretaker even remembered her sitting alone in the 5,000-seat amphitheater to watch the sunset. Earlier that day some of the same witnesses reported seeing a lone male around 50 years of age in the park "just standing around."

She was found the next day with a .38 caliber bullet in her head. This crime scene was different from the others in that Alderson was raped, then permitted to get dressed before being murdered. She was found propped, face up, against a rock with her right earring missing. Investigators believed that "her twisted arrangement" indicated that she may have been forced to kneel as well before being shot.

Mark McDermand—A Red Herring

Police thought they had the person responsible for her death when they investigated a double homicide on 16 October 1980, near Mount Tamalpais in Mill Valley. Mark McDermand, 35, and his brother, Edwin, 40, both lived with their mother, Helen, 75. At approximately 8:30 p.m. deputies responded to a call by a concerned friend. After forcing their way into the home, deputies found the body of a man lying in a hallway who was identified as Edwin. He had been shot in the head and chest. In a locked bedroom deputies found the deceased body of Helen, lying on the bed and covered by a blanket. She had a single bullet hole behind her left ear. Eight spent .22 caliber casings were found near the bodies.

Deputies found a small padlocked door that led to the basement. They discovered a note tacked to the inside of the door addressed to "Shitheels" that said that by the time the note and bodies were discovered it would be "way too late" and that the perpetrator would be found either "on the news or on a 'slab'". The note was signed "Mr. Hate."

Inside the room were spent .38 caliber casings, three .22 caliber bullets, and ankle holsters for a pistol and a knife. This smelly basement room had been Mark McDermand's bedroom and became the prime suspect.

The coroner said that the bodies had been dead for three or four days.

A few days later, the local newspaper and the Marin County Sheriff's Department received letters from an individual claiming responsibility for the double homicide and a handwriting expert stated that the same person who wrote the note at the McDermand's house also wrote these letters. In these letters, the writer stated that he would not be captured alive so on 24 October detectives devised a plan to lure him by running an ad directed at him with a phone number that said that if he surrendered he would be treated fairly.

McDermand called the number that evening and said that he was considering surrendering but that "he had some things to do first." He called again two days later with details about the murders; saying that he tried to kill his mother and brother quickly but miscalculated with Edwin, hence the multiple gunshot wounds. He said that he had to "stop Edwin from hurting others" and that he would turn himself in the next day.

When McDermand approached the police he was wearing a belt with a .38 caliber revolver and also had a set of thumb cuffs and three speed loaders. In his vehicle was a 12-gauge shotgun, a .22 caliber pistol, ammunition, a metal box containing several hypodermic syringes, and some insulin as McDermand was diabetic.

He told police that his brother was schizophrenic and had been deteriorating quickly so he borrowed the guns and then prepared to go on the run after the deed was done. McDermand said that he acted out of diminished capacity and that he, too, was schizophrenic and couldn't remember the murders or when he did he told several different stories.

Nevertheless, the jury found McDermand guilty of two counts of first-degree murder and he received the death penalty.

At the end of it all, investigators resolved his potential part in the trailside murders as none of his firearms matched the bullets found in the victims on Mount Tampalpais. That and the fact that the murders continued.

Shauna May

On 27 November 1980 25-year-old Shauna May disappeared from Point Reyes National Seashore Park while hiking. She was supposed to meet friends the following day to do more hiking. They had selected this area because it was several miles north of San Francisco and had not had the dubious distinction of having had a murder occur there recently. When she failed to show up, her friends alerted park officials.

Two days later her body was found by hikers who had seen her foot protruding from a shallow grave. She had been strangled with picture frame wire, shot three times in the head, and shoved into a shallow trench. She had also been raped.

Her body was found in close proximity to Diane O'Connell.

Diane O'Connell

The body of 22-year-old Diane O'Connell was found the same day and near May's body. She had disappeared a month earlier from the same area while hiking with friends as well and her body was rather decomposed. She had been raped, strangled with wire, and shot once in the head.

It was initially believed that the two women perhaps knew each other and were killed at around the same time as another hiker reported hearing four gunshots in that area of the park during the mid-afternoon.

The two women were laying together, face down. Their collective clothing was piled atop a backpack. A pair of underwear was stuffed into O'Connell's mouth. After investigating, it was determined that the two women did not know each other.

Richard Stowers and Cynthia Moreland

As if finding two bodies wasn't bad enough, police also discovered the bodies of 19-year-old Richard Towers and his girlfriend, 18-year-old Cynthia Moreland on the same day as May's and O'Connell's. The couple had been missing since 11 October, having last been seen by friends who they told that they were going to go hiking in the park. In fact, Stowers was in the Coast Guard and was reported as being AWOL.

Both victims had been murdered execution-style with bullets to the head.

An autopsy placed their time of death mere days before Alderson's, thus suggesting that there were two murderers or that a single killer had gone hunting for victims in two different areas. When ballistics determined that the bullet from Alderson's head matched those in both Stowers and Moreland, authorities knew there was just one single deadly predator.

Visitors were told not to go hiking alone; however, being together did not save Stowers and Moreland. Those who typically frequented the parks stayed away or went elsewhere until the murderer was caught.

Needless to say, the media frenzy that ensued wreaked panic throughout the area.

Was David Carpenter the Elusive Zodiac Killer?

Between December 1968 and July 1969 a man shot two couples on two separate occasions in Vallejo, California and then taunted detectives with phone calls claiming responsibility. One of the victims survived and was able to give police a description. Soon thereafter, editors of three San Francisco newspapers each received part of a strange letter also claiming to be from the killer. His message "consisted of a printed cryptogram composed of symbols and signed with a crossed-circle symbol" and all three of the letters had to be put together to decipher it. A local teacher was able to crack the code which stated that the killer enjoyed killing and it was his intention to continue doing so. He signed his letter "the Zodiac."

On 27 September 1969, while 20-year-old Bryan Hartnell and 22-year-old Cecelia Ann Shepard were picnicking at Lake Berryessa, a man in a black executioner's hood approached them. He stabbed Shepard ten times—five in the front and five in the back—and Hartnell six times in the back. He then called the police to report it.

Two weeks later the killer struck again, killing cab driver Paul Stine. The *San Francisco Chronicle* received a letter soon after accompanied by a torn piece of the shirt Stine was wearing at the time of his death. Investigators developed a number of suspects but none checked out. This serial killer was very clever and turned his escapades into multilayered games before he withdraw and maintained a low profile. This was quite disturbing for investigators who never knew when or where he would resurface.

In 1980, former FBI profiler John Douglas—who had been on the Zodiac case since it began—assisted sex crimes expert Special Agent Roy Hazelwood and San Francisco police to help create a profile of the Trailside Killer.

After examining the crime scene data and photos, Douglas concluded that the killer would be a local man who was shy, reclusive, and may have a speech impediment. Douglas also added that the murderer was likely socially awkward, white, intelligent, blue collar, and had spent time incarcerated. He was presumed to choose his victims out of opportunity rather than hunting the same type of victim. His modus operandi (MO) was to approach from behind and overwhelm his victim—"like a spider waiting for a bug to fly into his web." Douglas added that the killer would also have at least two of three specific background indicators common to many serial killers: bedwetting, fire-starting, and cruelty to animals. Finally, Douglas had said while the suspect likely committed rape in his past he had not killed anyone before his current murderous rampage. When questioned about the very specific speech impediment predictor, Douglas said that the secluded killing areas and method of approach indicated some type of shyness and/or shame and he believed it was due to some physical malady that really bothered the killer. Therefore, he attacked in the way he did to compensate for his handicap. While being very detailed, however, police still didn't have any potential suspects.

After Douglas returned to Quantico the Trailside Killer struck again.

Carpenter was ultimately cleared of any involvement with the Zodiac murders through fingerprint and handwriting analysis.

Ellen Hansen

On 29 March 1981, University of California at Davis undergraduate students Ellen Hansen and her boyfriend Stephen Haertle were ambushed in Henry Cowell State Park near Santa Cruz; another town that experienced a spate of murders during the early 1970s committed by Edmund Kemper, John Linley Frazier, and Herbert Mullin—all of whom were safely incarcerated at that time.

Carpenter approached the couple with a pistol in his hand and threatened the pair, insisting that Hansen permit him to rape her. Of course she refused, telling him off. Carpenter then opened fire, shooting Hansen point blank in the head twice and once in the shoulder. The assailant then shot Haertle and left him for dead. Haertle crawled for help despite wounds that ripped through his neck, a hand, and one eye. He proved instrumental in providing police with a partial description of the murderer: near 50, balding, approximately five-foot-ten to six-feet tall and approximately 170 pounds, with crooked yellow teeth, wearing dark glasses as well as a gold jacket with lettering on the back and a baseball cap. Haertle also remembered that the assailant had spoken in "quick, commanding sentences." This description differed considerably from the description of the Marin County killer; however, the MO was the same.

Other hikers reported that they had seen a man matching the description of the gunman in a red, late model, foreign car, running through the park after the gunshots had been fired.

Investigators were also able to lift some good shoeprint impressions to compare to a suspect when they got one.

Authorities released a composite drawing based upon Haertle's and other witness' descriptions in a number of newspapers to both alert people and hopefully get some leads. Four days later a woman called to describe a man she had met 26 years earlier on a cruise to Japan. She said that the purser on the cruise was a young man named David Carpenter who had been bothering her and her daughter with inappropriate behavior. She also recalled that he stuttered.

Presumably reading the paper and staying abreast with detectives' search for the Trailside Killer, Carpenter decided to grow a beard.

He then decided to kill much closer to home, enabling police to catch him.

Heather Scaggs

On 1 May 1981 police caught a break; however, it would come with another victim. On that day, 20-year-old Heather Scaggs disappeared on her way en route to buy a car with help from a coworker, one David Carpenter; they both worked at Econo Quick Print. She had told her boyfriend, Dan Pingle, that Carpenter "made a special point" of asking her to come alone when she came by to get the car and that his friend was selling it and Carpenter was going to help her purchase it. It was Pingle who informed police that she was missing. Luckily Scaggs had left Carpenter's address and phone number with him.

Scaggs' decomposing body was found on 24 May 1981 in Big Basin Redwood State Park, north of San Francisco. Ballistics from recovered bullets proved that she had been murdered with the same pistol used on Haertle and Hansen. She had also been raped and the DNA from the semen inside of her matched Carpenter.

Anna Menjivas

On 16 June 1981 a jaw bone later identified as belonging to Anna Menjivas was found by rock climbers in Castle Rock State Park. She had been missing since 28 December 1980 and was 17 years old at the time of her disappearance. She had worked part-time at the bank where Carpenter was a client and he often struck up conversation with her. Many believed that he only came into the bank to talk to her. Because the cause of death could not be established and there was scant evidence against him, he was not charged for her murder even though authorities were certain that he had killed her. Her name was added to the list of Carpenter's victims to bring his total to ten murders.

Investigation and Arrest

When police went to Carpenter's house to question him, they couldn't help but notice that Carpenter looked quite like the man in the composite sketch and that he had a shiny red Fiat.

Police discovered that Carpenter had not shown up on any released inmates' records where they initially searched due to a technicality: that he had been released by the state of California to serve a federal sentence and, while out on parole, was technically in federal custody. This issue resulted in the delay and subsequent difficulty in identifying him. That he was a habitual sex offender was another important factor not fully documented in his records.

The police department and FBI set up a surveillance van outside the house at 36 Sussex Street in San Francisco where Carpenter lived with his aging parents and also followed him on his errands, especially when he associated with other known criminals. They approached Carpenter who was walking down the street one day with a shopping bag in his hand to apprehend him. Initially confused, Carpenter then asked for a lawyer; at this point he was told that he was under arrest, to which he, strangely, begged, "Please don't hurt me."

Officers executed a search warrant on Carpenters home and car and found books about local hiking trails and over 60 maps. They talked to Carpenter's former fiancée who told them that he claimed that the gold jacket he once owned was stolen around the time of the Hansen murder; thus circumstantially placing him at the scene where Haertle and Hansen were shot. Further, Carpenter's car matched the one described by the surviving victim and several witnesses, he had the same optometrist as another victim, he had the right distinctive type of clothing, he had a record for violent sex offenses, he suffered from explosive rage and tried to change his appearance with different glasses and facial hair, and he matched many descriptions witnesses gave as the man who had been seen in the area of multiple attacks.

Haertle picked Carpenter's mugshot as the man who shot him and killed his girlfriend. Out of seven more witnesses present at a lineup, six picked him out although not all of them were sure. Police also conducted a car lineup with witnesses identifying Carpenter's Fiat.

He was formally charged with Hansen's murder and Haertle's attempted murder. At his arraignment Carpenter stuttered so badly that he had a difficult time answering the judges questions.

Police were never able to recover the .45 caliber gun that was used in several of his murders; however, a .38 caliber gun that Carpenter had sold to another man, who was on trial for robbery and gladly relinquished it to authorities, was later proven to be the firearm used in the last two murders.

Trial and Conviction

Carpenter's defense attorneys requested a change of venue due to the publicity surrounding his ten murders. However, if attorneys had thought it would make a difference they were mistaken. A change of venue would do nothing to eliminate the incriminating evidence police had against Carpenter. In April 1984, his Los Angeles trial began and on 6 July 1984, Carpenter was convicted of the Santa Cruz murders of Heather Scaggs and Ellen Hansen, and the attempted murder of

Stephen Haertle thanks to the damning evidence that his gun was the one responsible for their deaths. A second jury sentenced Carpenter to die in San Quentin's gas chamber based upon three special circumstances that warranted the death penalty: that he had committed multiple murders; that he had murdered during commission of rape; and that he had lain in wait for his victims. Judge Dion Morrow told the court that, "The defendant's entire life has been a continuous expression of violence and force almost beyond exception. I must conclude with the prosecution that if ever there was a case appropriate for the death penalty, this is it."

Carpenter's second trial began on 5 January 1988 in San Diego. On 10 May 1988, a San Diego jury found Carpenter guilty for five murders. Carpenter was also found guilty of two counts of rape and one count of attempted rape. This trial was different in that Carpenter himself took the stand in his own behalf. He was on the stand for seven days.

Marin County District Attorney Jerry Herman announced that he wouldn't file any charges against Carpenter for Kane's and Schwartz's murders due to inadequate evidence.

In 1994, potential juror misconduct in the second trial was brought to light in that the jury forewoman had known about Carpenter's convictions in Los Angeles for the Santa Cruz murders and had concealed this fact during voir dire for the Marin County trial. Carpenter was not retried as he had already been sentenced to death for other murders. On 6 March 1995 the California Supreme Court refused to give Carpenter a new trial. Justice Armand Arabian said that it was virtually impossible to keep secrets in cases such as this and that he believed that the juror's knowledge had not unduly biased the jury.

In 1997, the California Supreme Court upheld Carpenter's death sentence for the Scaggs and Hansen murders and on 29 November 199 they upheld Carpenter's death penalty from his second trial, with six of the seven justices agreeing that he had a fair trial for the five Marin County murders and had, in fact, been sentenced properly.

In December 2009, San Francisco police reexamined evidence from the 21 October 1979 murder of Mary Frances Bennett. Bennett was 23 years old at the time she was killed. She had been jogging near the Palace of the Legion of Honor in Land's End Park in San Francisco when she was ambushed and stabbed to death. Police reported that she had been stabbed at least 25 times in her chest, neck, and back. Her "butchered" corpse was found under a thin layer of dirt and leaves. In February 2010 San Francisco police confirmed that DNA collected from that murder was sent to the Department of Justice and was subsequently matched to Carpenter.

He remains a suspect in the murders of Edna Kane and Barbara Schwartz.

Aftermath

Some have speculated that Carpenter wasn't technically a serial killer but a serial rapist who killed his victims to eliminate witnesses so as not to return to prison.

Carpenter's case provided the background for Joyce Maynard's 2013 novel, *After Her*.

A series of geocaching caches have been placed throughout Mount Tamalpais in commemoration of Carpenter's victims.

THE TOY BOX KILLER

TERRY CAINE

David Parker Ray was a suspected American serial killer and known torturer and serial rapist of women; suspected because no bodies were ever found. However, he was accused by his accomplices of murdering a number of women and law enforcement officials estimate that he is responsible for as many as 60 deaths in and near Truth or Consequences, New Mexico. Ray purchased and refitted a trailer into what he called his "toy box" which was replete with a number of sex toys and torture items for his victims. He also played a very disturbing audiotape for all of his victims explaining what they will be enduring at his hand. Ray was finally arrested after one of his victims managed to escape after three days of torture. Ray stood trial for kidnapping and sexual torture and was sentenced to 224 years in prison; however, he suffered a fatal heart attack while incarcerated at Lea County Correctional Facility in Hobbs, New Mexico, on 28 May 2002.

Early Life

David Parker Ray was born on 6 November 1939, in Belen, New Mexico. He was named David after his uncle David who was accidentally shot in the heart at the age of 13 by his 15-year-old brother Alden just one year earlier. Ray's grandmother believed him to be a reincarnation of her dead son.

Ray's father, Cecil, was an alcoholic and was very abusive to both Ray and his sister Peggy—who was one year his junior—as well as their mother, Nettie. When Ray was ten years old his father left his mother and moved to Albuquerque. They were divorced soon thereafter. When Nettie decided to stay with her own parents, Ray and Peggy were shipped off to their paternal grandparents, Ethan and Dolly Ray. In the six years Ray and Peggy lived with their grandparents they saw their father twice and their mother only a handful of times. Consequently, there were no maternal bonds between Nettie and her children. In fact, Ray said that he didn't get much affection or attention at all during his childhood.

Ethan was a strict disciplinarian who insisted on the utmost standards of dress and behavior and, as such, the children were required to do ranch chores both before and after school and even though the Rays were not very well off, Ethan made sure his grandchildren were clean and presentable. He was also a devout fundamentalist Christian and made sure to instill within his grandchildren his religious beliefs. Any nonadherence to his rules resulted in physical punishment.

Ray attended Mountainair High School in Mountainair, New Mexico, where he was often bullied for his awkwardness and shyness, especially around girls. Ray commented that he didn't have his first date until he was 18 years old. He was also tormented for being soft-spoken and for having to keep his shirt buttoned all the way to the top—per his grandfather's instructions—when all of the other boys had a few top buttons undone. Ray was also a poor student.

Neighbor Audie Miranda always tried to look out for Ray. He would tell the bullies to leave him alone and stated that even though Ray could defend himself, he remained docile, not liking or believing in violence which was ironic considering what Ray would become. The two became close friends and spent a lot of time together on the Ray ranch riding horses, playing cowboys and Indians, and playing desert hide-and-seek.

Ray always had a love of the outdoors.

Miranda would later say that he believed that Ray's ultra-strict upbringing took a toll on his friend. Miranda even commented that he, himself, was scared of Ethan.

Dolly was not much better. Ray said that he hated her and that she "didn't have a clue."

At the age of 12, Ray began building and setting off bombs and other explosives he fashioned in the woods behind his grandparents' house. He said he blew up a lot of tree stumps as a child.

When Ray was 13 his grandparents gave him a Cushman Pacemaker motor scooter. He discovered within himself a natural aptitude for mechanics and delighted in taking it apart and then reassembling it. The once shy and timid Ray became more confident, especially when his classmates who used to torment him needed his services to fix their scooters.

Some accounts state that Ray began to use and abuse alcohol and drugs while in high school. It was also around this time he began to fantasize about raping, torturing, and murdering women. He said that the few times his father would come visit them, he would bring true detective magazines which Ray enjoyed reading. He began having his fantasies which always involved broken bottles. His sister stumbled upon Ray's sadomasochistic drawings as well as erotic photographs of acts of bondage.

At the age of 15 Ray fashioned his own little dungeon under a large piñon pine tree with a hangman's noose and a collection of broken beer bottles he "planned to use on girls someday." He also admitted to digging a hole and engaging in intercourse with the ground when he was lonesome.

After high school, Ray worked as an auto mechanic.

He married in 1959, joking that he was practically a virgin at that time, and joined the United States Army a year later where he was sent to Korea. The Rays had a son in 1960 and Ray had to return home on emergency leave because his wife was leaving the baby alone when she went out to party. He filed for divorce and sought sole custody. His mother, Opel, and stepfather, Cecil, raised Ray's son until Ray was honorably discharged from the military.

Ray married a second time in 1962 when he was 22 years old and a mere 90 days later he went back to court and filed for divorce again because they just didn't "click".

In 1966, Ray married a third time; to a woman named Glenda Burdine. They were married 15 years and had a daughter named Glenda Jean—who would go by "Jesse"—in 1969. Jesse remembered her father as being gone quite a bit, having worked for the railroad, and of having an unusual fetish for padded leather straps and other bondage fare. She said that kids were naturally curious and while they knew about it, it was not a topic to be discussed.

In sum, Ray married four times, was divorced four times, and had two children.

Ray met Cindy Lea Hendy in 1997 when he was 57; she was 20 years his junior. Originally from Washington, Hendy and her boyfriend John Youngblood moved to Truth or Consequences, New Mexico, on the run from the law for grand theft, forgery, and drug offenses, leaving her three children behind. As she had already served time in jail, she was not keen on returning.

The Crimes

The "Toy Box"

Ray spent over $100,000 on his homemade torture chamber he called his "toy box" that he constructed inside of an old white 15-feet-by-25-feet cargo trailer on his Elephant Butte, New Mexico, property. Elephant Butte is a resort town of approximately 2,000 residents, located along an 18-mile-long, 36,000-acre reservoir.

The trailer was stocked with what he referred to as his "friends": bully whips, pulleys, leather straps, metal clamps, bars which spread the victim's legs, surgical knifes and saws which he used to torture women. Inside this trailer were also numerous sex toys, syringes, detailed diagrams that showed different methods for inflicting pain and torture, and a homemade electrical generator. Ray also mounted a mirror on the ceiling above the gynecologist table upon which he strapped his victims because he wanted them to see everything that was done to them.

He also played a recorded audiotape of himself for his victims whenever they regained consciousness. It began with:

*"Hello there, b*tch. Are you comfortable right now? I doubt it. Wrists and ankles chained. Gagged. Probably blind folded. You are disoriented*

*and scared, too, I would imagine. Perfectly normal, under the circumstances. For a little while, at least, you need to get your sh*t together and listen to this tape. It is very relevant to your situation. I'm going to tell you, in detail, why you have been kidnapped, what's going to happen to you and how long you'll be here. I don't know the details of your capture, because this tape is being created July 23rd, 1993, as a general advisory tape for future female captives. The information I'm going to give you is based on my experience dealing with captives over a period of several years. If, at a future date, there are any major changes in our procedures, the tape will be upgraded. Now, you are obviously here against your will, totally helpless, don't know where you're at, don't know what's gonna happen to you. You're very scared or very pissed off. I'm sure that you've already tried to get your wrists and ankles loose, and know you can't. Now you're just waiting to see what's gonna happen next."*

The rest of the tape involves Ray setting forth his "rules" and "procedures" by telling his victims everything—in graphic detail—that would be done to them to include being raped and sodomized by Ray and his friends, engaging in bestiality, being shocked with electricity, and being poked and prodded with a multitude of surgical instruments and sex toys; essentially, being their sex slave to do with whatever they want. The actual recording is widely available online, quite long, and not for the faint of heart as it is extremely explicit.

In the audiotape Ray describes himself as a "dungeon master" who was affiliated with the Church of Satan and that his slaves were for members of his "congregation."

There was also a videotape showing Ray and his girlfriend Cindy Lea Hendy performing such acts of torture upon a female victim who screamed the entire time.

Psychological torture was also important to Ray. He would blindfold his victims, subject them to brainwashing, use fear tactics, and occasional small favors to keep them "off balance".

Many experts classify Ray as a sexual sadist who finds excitement and pleasure from inflicting pain upon a nonconsensual, submissive and inducing them into altered states of consciousness such as when they pass out from the pain. Such a predilection often forms during adolescence; however, experts do not know exactly what causes one to become a sexual sadist.

Ray had multiple accomplices during this time; including, allegedly, several of his girlfriends, particularly his latest girlfriend, Hendy.

During the investigation Hendy allegedly had told a friend—while she was under the influence of alcohol—that she had willingly participated in Ray's attacks because of the adrenaline rush she got from them. She allegedly confided to this person that "there were four to six people who had been killed, dismembered, and tossed into Elephant Butte Lake." While the friend did not initially believe her, after Ray and Hendy were arrested and the details of the crimes were released, he gave statements to police and the media.

Marie Parker

On 5 July 1997, 22-year-old Marie Parker and her two daughters—ages four and five—were evicted from their apartment for non-payment of rent. They were living in a pup tent on the western shore of Elephant Butte Lake at a campsite called Hot Springs Cove; just north of Ray's trailer. In fact, she had borrowed the tent from him and when her campsite became too messy for the fastidious Ray, he had something to say about it.

Parker was a methamphetamine and cocaine junkie and her main supplier was Ray's daughter Jesse. Ray abducted Parker and took her to his toy box where he raped and tortured her for three days after which he gave Yancy a rope and told him that they "were finished" with her. He then told Yancy to kill her which Yancy admitted to doing. They buried the body in a remote area and Ray threatened Yancy's life if he ever told anyone.

Later, when police took Yancy to the area where Parker's body was allegedly dumped, they could not find any evidence. Yancy stated that Ray probably moved the body.

Police found Parker's abandoned car in the parking lot of the Blue Waters Saloon.

Cynthia Vigil

Cynthia Vigil had been working as a prostitute along Central Avenue (Highway 66) at around 10:00 a.m. when her pimp introduced her to Ray and Hendy in a red recreational vehicle. Ray offered Vigil $20 for oral sex and when she entered the vehicle, Ray produced a police badge and told Vigil that she was under arrest for solicitation. Ray and Hendy handcuffed, gagged, and chained Vigil to a fixture inside of the camper. After a few minutes he pulled the vehicle over and then proceeded to cut off all of her clothing, put a metal dog collar around her neck, place her in shackles, and then slipped a leather mask over her head with no eye openings and a zipper for the mouth. She was also told if she resisted she would be shocked.

When they reached Ray's house, after driving for an hour, Vigil said that she was chained to a bed and was made to listen to Ray's infamous five-minute audiotape before being forced to have sex with both Ray and Hendy. Next, Vigil said that Ray put gravy "up" her and had his German shepherd lick it off. Vigil then had her knees attached to a bar, forcing her legs open and was then "measured" with dildoes that had markings on them before having her breasts and genitals shocked with a portable generator. The entire time Hendy had a gun pointed at her.

The next morning, Vigil was taken at gunpoint to the bathroom to relieve herself and then taken back to the bed, fresh and clean white sheets atop it, where her mouth and eyes were duct taped and she was hog-tied with an elaborate collection of interconnected leather straps. A rope was then attached to a pulley from the ceiling and Vigil's entire body was lifted three feet into the air.

The duct tape was ripped from her eyes and she saw her horrified face staring back at her from a video monitor. She said that Ray tied her legs open and proceeded to whip her with a leather belt, whips, and a cat-o' nine tails. Vigil said that the beating excited Ray who then violated her with a "horrendous looking dildo" and took pictures of her suspended body with the toys inside of her.

Later that day he attached an elaborate system of clamps and pulleys to her breasts and genitalia and proceeded to shock her. Her convulsions caused the pulleys to exert force on the clamps. After taking the excruciating pain for as long as she could, she lost consciousness.

For the next two days Vigil was subjected to sexual torture until she was able to escape.

On 22 March 1999, Cynthia Vigil escaped after being abducted by Ray and enduring a three-day torture ordeal. She was able to escape one morning after Ray had left for work and Hendy had left the keys on a nearby table when the latter went into another room to talk on the phone. Vigil—chained to the wall in the den—managed to use her legs and feet to pull the table toward her and get the keys; however, Hendy noticed her efforts and a fight ensued. Vigil was able to free herself while Hendy beat her and even after being hit in the head with a lamp, Vigil managed to stab Hendy in the back of the neck with an icepick she found on the floor. When Hendy fell to the ground, Vigil escaped the house naked save for an iron slave collar and padlocked chains, and began to run down Bass Road in Elephant Butte. Since she had just been taken three days ago, Vigil had not been taken out to the toy box yet.

Vigil was spotted by a couple of passing motorists who did not know what to make of the woman and didn't stop. Vigil finally surprised a woman at home in her trailer watching television who called the police for her. Vigil was then taken to the Sierra Vista

County Hospital emergency room where the chains were cut off and her battered body was cared for.

When police went to Ray's home, they found bloodied sheets in one bedroom with a broken lamp and broken window, thus corroborating Vigil's claims. A pulley device with hooks and chains was mounted on the ceiling and there was a long, coffin-like box along the side of the bed. Large sex toys were on the dresser.

Arrest and Investigation

After Vigil's escape, Ray and Hendy were arrested off Springfield Road in his red Toyota camper. They claimed that they had kidnapped Vigil in an effort to break her of her heroin addiction. Ray and Hendy were taken to nearby Truth or Consequences—formerly Hot Springs—New Mexico and housed in the Cooper Police Training Center.

Both Ray and Hendy were charged with 12 counts consisting of aggravated kidnapping, conspiracy, and aggravated battery and held on $1 million bail.

Soon after Ray was arrested, New Mexico State Police took the case over from the Truth or Consequences Police Department and Agent Wesley LaCuesta—a five-year veteran of the Criminal Assault and Violent Crimes Division—was called on to assist in the investigation. He left his Las Cruces office and headed north to Truth or Consequences.

LaCuesta interviewed Vigil at the hospital. He observed many small cuts on her extremities, injuries to her breasts, welts on her back, and evidence of her being handcuffed.

By early April 1999, over 100 New Mexico State Police and FBI agents were all over Ray's property looking for human remains.

Eleven days after his arrest, Patty Rust committed suicide after assisting law enforcement personnel with detailed drawings of the toy box over the course of four days. Prosecutor Jim Yontz wondered why the FBI would send a woman into a torture chamber where many women had likely been frightened to death by Ray and the torture he inflicted upon them. He then went to visit the toy box. Inside he found a ghastly collection of sex toys, medical devices, whips, clamps, chains, pulleys, rods, saws, and other items for bondage and sadomasochism; in addition to detailed drawings of how Ray liked to torture his victims, medical books on the female anatomy, and, perhaps most damning, a videotape dating back to 1993 showing a woman being tortured.

There was also a television monitor in the right corner of the toy box so Ray's victims could see what he was doing to them if they looked at the monitor while they were secured to the table. He also had a video camera focused upon the table recording everything he was doing. Photographs of the torture he had inflicted upon prior victims decorated the walls, as well as a bunch of dolls which were "strung up in various states of bondage and torture." In addition to the medical texts, Ray had a copy of Brett Easton Ellis' *American Psycho*; a novel detailing violent assaults inflicted by a man when he needed to release steam from his high-stress life that was also made into a film starring Christian Bale. The novel contains very disturbing descriptions of torture. It was presumed that Ray compared himself to the "protagonist" in the novel as he saw himself as in control and his victims as "expendable pawns in his game", even going so far as to call his victims "packages."

With respect to the videotape depicting the torture of one of Ray's victims, the police were able to find the woman on the tape: Kelly Garrett, who had been married mere days before being abducted by Ray and Hendy. Garrett had been held hostage, raped, and tortured for three days before being drugged and left on the side of the road not far from her in-laws' house. Believing Garrett had been out on a drug binge, she was asked to leave and subsequently moved back to Colorado. Investigators found her in Colorado and she stated that she had amnesia for a long time, only recently—as in the past year—remembering what Ray and Hendy had done to her.

The publicity surrounding the case prompted another victim to come forward with her story. Angelica Montano recounted her ordeal at Ray's hands just one month ago.

Angelica Montano

Montano said that she was a casual acquaintance of both Ray and Hendy and had gone to their house on 17 February 1999, looking to borrow cake mix. She said that Ray left the room and then returned with a knife and told her that she was being kidnapped. When Montano looked over at Hendy, she saw the woman holding a gun, pointed at her. She knew they were serious.

Montano said that the couple grabbed, bound, and stripped her before strapping her to a bed and placing a metal collar on her. She said they then attached electrodes to her breasts and shocked her multiple times in addition to "abus[ing] her with various sexual implements." She then said that Ray forced her to give him oral sex.

After having been chained naked to the bed for three days and being subjected to sexual abuse, it was time for Montano to visit the toy box. Ray removed her handcuffs and led her to the bathroom with a long metal leash attached to the dog collar. He bathed her "like a dog, with a chain and everything" Montano would later say. When she was clean, Hendy applied makeup to her face and then draped a robe over her captive's shoulders before Ray and Hendy led her out into the trailer.

In the smaller trailer—the toy box—Montano was strapped to a gynecologist table where she was subjected to additional electric shocks to her genitalia as well as other instances of sexual assault. She said that she repeatedly begged Ray and Hendy to release her and on the fourth day they relented. She was drugged and taken miles away from Ray's property and dumped on a local highway in the desert where a police officer found her.

Even though Montano did, in fact, report the incident to the police, there had been no follow up. When she saw that Ray and Hendy had been arrested, Montano contacted the police again.

Accomplices

In addition to Hendy, investigators discovered two other accomplices: Ray's daughter Glenda Jean "Jesse" Ray; and Dennis Roy Yancy. Yancy and Hendy had dated in the past.

Yancy admitted to strangling Marie Parker—a former girlfriend—after Ray kidnapped and tortured her. Ray videotaped the murder. Yancy also confessed to seeing photographs of one of Ray's ex-wives in various bondage positions as well as watching Ray torture a woman inside the toy box but that he thought it was consensual. Yancy was subsequently convicted of second-degree murder and conspiracy to commit first-degree murder. He received two 15-year sentences. Jesse was also tried and convicted of kidnapping for sexual torture. She was sentenced to seven years and served three, the rest of the time she was on parole.

Hendy was charged with 25 felonies and was looking at 197 years in prison. To save herself, she agreed to plead no contest and testify against Ray and Yancy in exchange for five felony counts and a 36-year sentence. In the Seventh District Court of New Mexico Hendy pled guilty to two counts of first-degree kidnapping for Vigil and Montano, two counts of sexual penetration (rape) in the second degree for the two women, and one count of conspiracy to commit second-degree kidnapping.

Over 100 FBI agents were sent to search Ray's property but they were unable to identify any human remains. Several bones were located but they proved to be of animal origin. Collecting evidence from Ray's home and toy box proved daunting due to the sheer number of items he had amassed for his tortuous pleasure. In one interview, New Mexico Public Safety Director Darren White told reporters that the evidence inside the toy box was "very disturbing stuff" and "literally made my stomach turn."

It was later discovered that Ray would drug his victims with sodium pentothal and phenobarbital to induce amnesia to prevent them from being able to report what had happened to them when they were released. In Kelly Garrett's case, she was unsure about her own recollections of the torture and accompanying nightmares; that is, until the FBI contacted her and, soon thereafter, she was able to remember—in vivid detail—what Ray did to her so she could testify against him in court.

In his recording, Ray described his whole philosophy about drugging his victims and why getting an accurate body count of those victims he killed is impossible. Ray said:

*"If I killed every b*tch that we kidnapped, there'd be bodies strung all over the country. And besides, I don't like killin' a girl, unless it is absolutely necessary. So I've devised a safe, alternate method of disposal. I had plenty of b*tches to practice on over the years, so I've pretty well got it down pat. And I enjoy doin' it. I get off on mind games. After we get completely through with you, you're gonna be drugged up real heavy, with a combination of Sodium Pentothal and Phenobarbital. They are both hypnotic drugs that will make you extremely susceptible to hypnosis, autohypnosis and hypnotic suggestion. You're gonna be kept drugged a couple of days, while I play with your mind. By the time I get through brainwashing you, you're not gonna remember a fu*kin' thing about this little adventure. You won't remember this place, us, or what has happened to you. There won't be any DNA evidence, because you'll be bathed, and both holes between your legs will be thoroughly flushed out. You'll be dressed, sedated, and turned loose on some country road, bruised, heh, sore all over, but nothing that won't heal up in a week or two. The thought of being brainwashed may not be appealing to you, but we been doin' it a long time and it works. And it's the lesser of two evils. I'm sure that you would prefer that, in lieu of being strangled or having your throat cut."*

One can only imagine the pure horror coursing through his victims' minds as they lay, chained atop his torture table, hearing—in very graphic detail—about what they will be enduring.

Trials and Convictions

The press jumped all over the case and soon discovered that everyone who seemingly knew Ray said that he seemed like a "regular" guy. He did not have any criminal record, nor were there any reports about potentially suspicious activities on his property which he leased from the park service. However, reports from the police indicated that he was considerably worse and darker than he initially seemed.

State District Judge Neil Mertz decided that Ray would undergo three separate trials: for Cynthia Vigil, for Angelica Montano, and for Kelly Garrett. The Vigil trial was set to start on 28 March 2000, in Tierra Amarilla. Judge Mertz suppressed Ray's early interviews with the New Mexico State Police and FBI and also banned the media from the voir dire. Just after jury selection, Ray allegedly suffered a heart attack and was taken to a hospital in Las Cruces. The judge postponed the trial for another week and then there were additional delays and several FBI expert witnesses were excluded.

Then, unexpectedly, Judge Mertz decided to start Garrett's trial for her 1996 kidnapping and torture even though it was the weakest case, evidence-wise. Nevertheless, Judge Mertz scheduled it for the end of May. Of course, Ray was pleased with the delays, not to mention Judge Mertz's exclusion of Ray's printed sheet of procedures for handling his slaves as well as all devices found in the trailer for Garrett's trial since nobody could prove they were there in 1996. This left the prosecution with the videotape and the victim's testimony.

When Vigil's trial was actually conducted, it ended in a mistrial because some jurors were not convinced that the women were completely held against their will and there was a subsequent retrial that resulted in convictions for all 12 counts with which Ray was charged.

Montano's trial was delayed indefinitely because, unfortunately, she was rushed to an Albuquerque hospital on 7 May 2001 with pneumonia where she died an hour later from heart failure. She was only 28 years old. As she was one of only three living, known witnesses who were going to testify against Ray, Montano's death dealt a huge blow to the prosecution. However, prosecutor Jim Yontz was prepared to try Ray for Montano's kidnapping and torture by utilizing videotaped statements she had made at a preliminary hearing on 15 and 16 April 1999.

When prosecutors started "closing in" on his daughter Jesse who assisted with some of Ray's earlier kidnappings, Ray decided to take a plea bargain. He received a sentence of 224 years in prison.

Ray suffered a fatal heart attack while incarcerated at Lea County Correctional Facility in Hobbs, New Mexico, on 28 May 2002.

Aftermath

Yancy was paroled in 2010 after serving 11 years of his sentence; however, his release was delayed because of difficulties stemming from his parole plan which had to be established before release. Three months after he was released in 2011, he was charged with violating his parole and subsequently returned to prison and required to serve his entire sentence until 2021.

Ray is suspected of murdering his one-time business partner, Billy Bowers. The two men bought, restored, and sold cars. On 22 September 1988, Bowers disappeared and his family immediately offered a $5,000 reward for any information leading to his safe return. On 28 September 1989, a fisherman found a male body floating in McCrea Canyon which is along the eastern shore of Elephant Butte Lake. The body was wrapped in a blue tarp and secured to two heavy boat anchors. It had a single bullet hole to the head and $49.47 in a pocket but no identification. There were no missing persons reports for a five-foot-ten-inch male in his late-30's or early-40's so the John Doe remained unidentified for over a decade until Cindy Hendy told police that Ray had murdered Bowers. Hendy admitted that Ray confessed the murder to her and told her that since then he had learned to open the victims' stomachs so they would "stay down" when submerged in water and not float to the surface as was the case with Bowers.

When the body was exhumed and dental records compared, the John Doe was, in fact, Bowers. His son Michael was able to retrieve the body of his long-lost father for a proper burial and some closure.

In November 2002, state police officially opened the toy box to the public in the hopes that renewed media attention might help identify additional victims. Inside were signs that said "Satan's Den" and "Bondage Room." The obstetrical table was still there with all of its clamps, leg stretchers, electric wires, chains, and straps. A steel cabinet held numerous surgical instruments and the coffin-shaped box used to terrorize and contain victims was nearby. Ray's meticulous records detailing what he did to his victims was also available. To ensure that none of his victims escaped, Ray had devised an elaborate alarm system and had written instructions to ensure that all straps were secure prior to leaving the toy box.

However, with Ray dead, the investigation went cold, especially since no bodies were ever found, no possible victims were identified, and no suspicious deaths which might have been loosely linked to Ray were solved. Despite the lack of any dead bodies, he is oft-labeled in numerous sources of literature as a serial killer.

According to Jim Fielder in his 2003 book *Slow Death*, both Vigil and Garrett went on to form relationships and start families of their own.

As recently as 2012, additional evidence has been uncovered which indicated there may be additional victims.